HOW TO DO YOUR OWN DIVORCE

WITHDRAWN

If you want to know how...

The Divorced Dad's Handbook
*Advice, support and guidance for all fathers
going through separation or divorce*

How to Deal with Death and Probate

The Carer's Handbook
Essential information and support for all those in a caring role

Life Talk for a Daughter
*Emotional wisdom and practical survival skills
on 60 of life's most significant issues*

howtobooks

Send for a free copy of the latest catalogue to:

How To Books
Spring Hill House, Spring Hill Road,
Begbroke, Oxford OX5 1RX. United Kingdom.
info@howtobooks.co.uk
www.howtobooks.co.uk

HOW TO DO YOUR OWN DIVORCE

A PRACTICAL STEP-BY-STEP GUIDE TO THE LEGAL
AND FINANCIAL PROCESSES IN THE BREAKDOWN OF MARRIAGE

PETER WADE

howtobooks

Published by How To Books Ltd,
Spring Hill House, Spring Hill Road,
Begbroke, Oxford OX5 1RX. United Kingdom.
Tel: (01865) 375794. Fax: (01865) 379162.
email: info@howtobooks.co.uk
http://www.howtobooks.co.uk

British Library Cataloguing in Publication Data
A catalogue record for this book is available from the British Library

ISBN 978 1 84528 151 9

Cover design by Baseline Arts Ltd, Oxford
Produced for How To Books by Deer Park Productions, Tavistock, Devon
Typeset by PDQ Typesetting, Newcastle-under-Lyme, Staffs.
Printed and bound by Bell & Bain Ltd, Glasgow

NOTE: The material contained in this book is set out in good faith for general guidance and no liability
can be accepted for loss or expense incurred as a result of relying in particular circumstances on
statements made in the book. The laws and regulations are complex and liable to change, and readers
should check the current position with the relevant authorities before making personal arrangements.

Contents

Introduction

Although this book is called *How to Do Your Own Divorce* it can be used in one of at least two ways. You can literally follow through the steps and complete the divorce without legal help from a solicitor. There are some straightforward cases, particularly where there are no children and the property issues are clear, where that would be possible.

It could also be used as a back-up for someone going through a divorce via a solicitor, so that they have a clear idea as to what stage they are at and what is going on. In these enlightened times it is impossible for professionals to keep the public in the dark. The internet is available and you can now effectively look up any information you wish.

In my experience as a practising solicitor the areas that can cause difficulty for anyone doing their own divorce without legal help would be property and children. Ultimately the court can settle the question of children. The difficulty is enforceability. There has been a lot of bad publicity about the rights of fathers. Even the best and most expensive lawyers in the land seem unable to resolve that one, so you may take the view that doing it yourself means that you will not have to pay the lawyer's bill.

LAYOUT OF THE BOOK

I have read a lot of books on divorce so that you do not have to. Many are confusing and my opinion is that there are some people out there who are very good at doing the job but cannot explain it to anyone else. My car mechanic is an expert at fixing my car but may not be an expert at telling me in clear, unambiguous language how they achieved that result and the theory behind it. In a way that suits me, as I don't really want to know, I just want my car to work.

I have tried to create a practical guide that cuts out as much extraneous comment as possible. Other divorce books aimed at the public have all the information you can possibly want but skate over some important practical issues. This means that all the clues are in there but you have to find them. The purpose of this book is provide a clear and easy to follow and practical guide to the subject of how to do your own divorce.

The layout of the book:

◆ the law;
◆ checklist of the practical steps;
◆ suggested letters;
◆ forms and example documents and how to fill them in.

If you wish therefore you can cut the chat and go straight to the checklist of practical steps and use the suggested letters and fill in the forms. I have tried to make each section as clear as possible. The only repetition will be with legal terminology. I will define what I am talking about then use the short form next time I refer to it.

Each chapter is self-contained and you will not have to keep going backwards and forwards throughout the book to find out what is going on. I have set myself a tough task and I hope by the end that you will have a clear guide to divorce with all the technicalities stripped away and described in clear language. If there are any ambiguities it will be entirely my fault.

Am I Entitled to a Divorce?

Before you can file for a divorce you must have been married for one year and one or both parties must be resident or domiciled in England or Wales.

If your situation fulfils both these conditions you should now choose a county court in England and Wales to file a petition for a divorce.

SEPARATION OR DIVORCE?

In a separation each spouse maintains his or her normal entitlements under the marriage agreement as it concerns their financial affairs.

As mentioned above, to get divorced you must have been married for more than one year, and one or both parties must be resident or domiciled in England and Wales. You must complete a form, called a petition, giving the reasons why you are applying for a divorce, and which shows that your marriage is definitely over. If you have children you should also complete a form called the statement of arrangements for children in which you tell the court what plans you have made for the children once the divorce is final.

Until the divorce and all financial matters have been resolved both parties are still legally married. People may wish to continue with a divorce rather than a separation so as to finalise their financial affairs. Once a *decree nisi* has been granted, and a consent order entered into, a full and final settlement is usually achieved and the party's financial affairs are now separate.

When the parties' divorce comes through and the consent order is entered into there can be no going back.

To continue with a simple divorce the following forms will be required:

- a copy of the marriage certificate;
- Form D8 (Petition) completed in triplicate if there are children;
- a statement of arrangements for children (Form D 8A (M4));
- if you are exempt from paying the fee Form EX160.

Then:

- the court will arrange to serve the petition on the respondent;
- Form D9H will be sent to you to confirm that the petition has indeed been served;
- the court will post to the respondent a form D10 acknowledgement of service together with a copy of the petition.

In only a tiny proportion of cases will divorce proceedings go to a full trial. Most cases are settled after brief directions hearings, or through negotiations at the court, without any evidence being given apart from that contained in the petition and with only a few questions asked to verify any controversial areas.

These sessions are usually held in chambers with no other parties present and they are fairly informal. This allows the facts to be put across in a conversational manner so that the parties can see what the judge wishes to know and the decisions the judge has come to.

THE LAW ON DIVORCE

There is only one ground for Divorce – the irretrievable breakdown of a marriage. This ground is contained in the Matrimonial Causes Act (MCA) 1973.

The evidence for the irretrievable breakdown of a marriage comes from one of five facts:

1. Fact A: adultery.
2. Fact B: behaviour.
3. Fact C: desertion.
4. Fact D: two years' separation with the consent of the respondent.
5. Fact E: five years' separation.

If one of these facts is proved the presumption is that the marriage has irretrievably broken down.

Fact A: adultery

To prove this fact there has to have been an act of adultery and the petitioner must now find it intolerable to live with the respondent. Adultery is defined as voluntary sexual intercourse between a married person and a person of the opposite sex, whether married or not, who is not that married person's spouse. From a practical point of view, the method of proof is a confession statement. A confession statement is now usually included on the acknowledgement of service.

Because the petitioner must also find it intolerable to live with the respondent, an act of adultery is only valid if the petition is filed within six months of the act being discovered.

Fact B: behaviour

There is no definition as to what constitutes unreasonable behaviour. The test for unreasonable behaviour is therefore subjective, that which a particular petitioner finds unreasonable.

Some examples of unreasonable behaviour include the following:

- violence;
- lack of communication;
- lack of socialising;
- neglect;
- bullying;
- constant criticism;
- financial irresponsibility;
- obsessive DIY;
- emotional dissatisfaction;
- sexual dissatisfaction;
- desertion;
- boredom and growing apart.

Fact C: desertion and constructive desertion

For this proof to hold there must be an actual separation and the respondent must have every intention to desert. Lack of consent to the separation by the petitioner and the separation is without just cause.

Facts D and E: separation

Fact D is two years' separation with respondent's consent. The parties must have lived apart continuously for a period of two years immediately preceding the presentation of the petition.

Fact E is five years' separation. This ground includes provision for grave financial hardship.

SPECIMEN GROUNDS FOR DIVORCE

This section contains examples of wording you could use in your petition, depending on your circumstances

Specimen particulars of adultery

The respondent has committed adultery and the petitioner now finds it intolerable to live with him or her.

It is no longer necessary to name the person with whom the adultery is alleged to have been committed.

> Since about [insert the date] the respondent has committed
> adultery at [if possible give full address] with the co-respondent.

If the co-respondent is unknown, the following particulars should be substituted:

> Since about [insert the date] the respondent has lived, cohabited
> and frequently committed adultery at [if possible, give full address]
> with a [man/woman] whose name and identity are unknown to the
> petitioner.

If the adultery has resulted in a child:

> On [insert the date], in consequence of the said adultery, the
> respondent was delivered of a child.

If the co-respondent has died the following particulars should be
substituted:

> On or about [insert the date] the respondent committed adultery at
> [address] with the co-respondent who subsequently died on
> [insert the date].

If a finding of previous adultery is relied on, and the petitioner
intends to cite evidence that the respondent was found guilty of
adultery in matrimonial proceedings between the co-respondent
and the co-respondent's wife at [court name] then the issue in
those proceedings was whether the co-respondent and respondent
had committed adultery together.

Where there has been a subsequent resumption of co-habitation:

> On [insert the date] the petitioner, with the knowledge of the
> respondent's said adultery, resumed cohabitation with her at
> [address], but the said resumption did not exceed six months, and
> on [insert the date] the parties have separated and have since then
> lived separately and apart.

Specimen particulars of intolerable behaviour

Assaults

The respondent has a bad temper and has frequently assaulted the
petitioner:

This is one example; on the [insert the date] when the petitioner was watching television the respondent struck him/her about the head and face with great force with the heel of [his/her] shoe.

On the day of [insert the date] when the petitioner was about to go to work, the respondent threw a large number of plates at [his/her] head and struck [his/her] face with a brush.

[He/she] threatened to stab [him/her] with the carving knife.

On the [insert the date] the respondent threatened to break the petitioner's head with a hammer saying [I will swing for you] then broke a glass coffee table with the hammer and said to the petitioner [that's what will happen to your head one of these days].

Drunkenness and insulting behaviour

The following example may apply in cases of drunkenness or insulting behaviour.

Throughout the marriage the respondent has drunk to excess causing considerable distress to the petitioner despite [her/his] requests for [her/him] to moderate [her/his] drinking.

When the respondent is intoxicated [he/she] is abusive to the petitioner and habitually uses obscene language in front of the children of the family causing them great distress.

The respondent has often vomited when drunk in various parts of the matrimonial home and the petitioner has on many occasions been obliged to clean up the mess. Also on several occasions the respondent has urinated in bed and in various parts of the bedroom as a result of [his/her] excessive drinking.

Failure to maintain

The following are grounds for failure to maintain.

Throughout the marriage the respondent has kept the petitioner short of housekeeping money and has on occasions too numerous to mention provided the petitioner with no housekeeping money at all. He is a habitual gambler and during the course of the marriage has continually distressed the petitioner by running up large betting losses.

The respondent has incurred large debts as a result of his reckless and extravagant spending and the petitioner has constantly found herself besieged by the respondent's creditors threatening to take proceedings in respect of the large debts.

The petitioner has regularly protested with the respondent about his behaviour and has begged him to reform but he has callously disregarded her entreaties, knowing the distressing effect his conduct is having on her.

Improper association

The following are grounds for improper association.

The respondent has persisted in an association with another [man/woman] [name] in such a way as to lead the petitioner to suspect that the said association is adulterous or, as the case may be, of a [lesbian/homosexual nature].

Excessive moodiness
Examples of excessive moodiness.

The respondent has since the [ ] day of [insert the date] frequently and habitually indulged in extreme fits of moodiness and silence which to his knowledge have isolated the petitioner from her and have caused her distress and anxiety.

The respondent will without warning and without cause suddenly cease to speak to the petitioner for unexplained reasons and will on such occasions cease to share the matrimonial bedroom with the petitioner and to have anything to do with her for lengthy periods of time.

On numerous occasions such periods of silence and moodiness have lasted for at least three weeks.

The respondent will also indulge in such fits of moodiness after trivial arguments about domestic matters.

As an example of the respondent's said behaviour the petitioner refers to one occasion on or about [insert the date] when the respondent complained to the petitioner that a button was missing from his shirt and did not speak to the petitioner for two weeks thereafter.

The petitioner has frequently told the respondent of the distress, which his said behaviour has caused to her but he has been completely indifferent to the complaints.

Excessive jealousy
The following are grounds for excessive jealousy.

Since the date of the marriage the respondent has displayed an unprovoked and irrational jealousy where the petitioner is concerned which has persisted despite the remonstrance of the petitioner and despite the adverse effect which to his knowledge the respondent's said jealousy has had on the petitioner.

The respondent frequently alleges without justification that the petitioner shows an interest in other men. He repeatedly suggests that she 'fancies' the milkman, the postman and the butcher. He used to watch the petitioner during the whole of the evening when at parties, and when out together on social occasions, and, invariably on their return to the matrimonial home, he accused her of 'fancying' another man.

On one occasion in or about [insert the date] the respondent wrongfully and to her great distress accused the petitioner of having an affair with the respondent's 17-year-old brother.

In consequence of the respondent's said conduct the petitioner became afraid to talk to any other men and to go out with the respondent socially. She lost sleep and had to consult a medical practitioner because of her state of anxiety.

She was prescribed tranquillisers. Because of the respondent's said conduct the petitioner was finally compelled to leave the respondent on the [insert the date].

DIVORCE PROCEDURE

There is no set legal format for the petition. The Family Proceeding Rules (1991) however set out what must be included.

- The names of the parties.
- The date and place of the marriage.
- The full names (including surnames) and dates of birth of any children.
- Details of any previous proceedings and assessments by the Child Support Agency.
- A statement that the marriage has irretrievably broken down.
- The fact relied upon for divorce.
- Particulars (but not evidence) of the matters relied upon to prove that fact.

The petition must also included the prayer to the court:

- That the marriage be dissolved.
- Any costs order sought.
- The financial relief required for the petitioner and/or the children.

The following documents are also required.

- The marriage certificate.
- The statement of arrangements for the children (see below).
- The reconciliation certificate, if appropriate. On this certification the solicitor indicates whether or not reconciliation has been discussed; he or she does *not* indicate whether a reconciliation has been attempted.
- The court fee or a certificate of exemption.

The statement of arrangements for the children

If practical, the statement of arrangements for the children form (form M4) should be agreed, and both parties should sign it to indicate their agreements to the arrangements. If the respondent refuses to sign the form it may still be filed, signed by the petitioner alone.

The form M4 covers:

♦ accommodation;
♦ education;
♦ child care arrangements;
♦ financial arrangements;
♦ contact for the non-residential partner;
♦ health.

Serving the petition once it is completed

The court will serve the petition through the post. The respondent will receive a copy of the petition and an acknowledgement of service, which has to be returned within a certain period.

In cases of adultery where a co-respondent has been named the petition is deemed to have been served.

Once the acknowledgement of service has been returned the petition is deemed to have been served. If the acknowledgement is not returned, a bailiff or other agency can serve the petition.

The petition contains various questions the respondent must answer:

- whether he or she consents to the divorce;
- whether he or she objects to the claims for costs;
- whether or not he or she wishes to make his or her own application for order of the children.

As mentioned earlier the only ground for a divorce is the irretrievable breakdown of a marriage. It is therefore very difficult to claim that the marriage is still in existence if one of the parties claims that the marriage has irretrievably broken down. It is possible however to cross-petition, and this must be filed within 29 days of the petition being served.

Decree nisi

The next stage of the divorce, once all the papers have been properly served, is the *decree nisi*.

After the acknowledgement has been returned, the petitioner completes an *affidavit*. When this has been sworn it is sent to the court with the application forms requesting directions for trial. The date is then fixed for the *decree nisi*.

The judge will give the following directions.

- If he or she is satisfied with the petition and affidavit they will certify that the petitioner is entitled to a decree nisi and a divorce, and a date will be fixed to pronounce the decree nisi.

- He or she will also consider whether the statement of arrangements for children is in order, and a certificate will be issued to that effect.

Decree Absolute

Six weeks and one day after the *decree nisi*, the *decree absolute* may be requested. Unless the petitioner is exempt from paying costs this will incur a fee of £30.

If however the petitioner does not apply for *decree nisi* or for a *decree absolute*, three months later the respondent may apply for the decree to be made absolute.

2

The Costs

LEGAL COSTS OR SOLICITORS' FEES?

Although the title of this book is *How to Do Your Own Divorce*, at some stage you will pay either the other side's costs or your solicitor for his or her services. It is therefore important to understand how legal costs are calculated, because costs are an important consideration in all divorces.

The Solicitors' Practice Rules state that solicitors must give as an accurate as possible breakdown of their potential fees (which solicitors call costs).

At the outset of the cases they must provide an estimate of the expenses they are likely to incur and of the financial risks involved.

There are other expenses, such as VAT and disbursements, which the Law Society have now told solicitors must be called out of pocket expenses. The costs a solicitor charges for doing the work are usually broken down into the time (the number of hours' work the case involved) taken, and the skills involved.

Solicitors' charges are usually expressed as an hourly rate, plus VAT, which is currently 17.5 per cent and which is paid on the total of the charges. That means any other expenses which you would have to pay even if you were conducting your own affairs such as court costs, searches, fees payable to third parties for their work such as experts, surveyors, valuers, etc.

Solicitors' fees

Solicitors' work is divided into contentious and non-contentious matters. Divorce is regarded as contentious because it can result in a court appearance. Because it is not possible to predict how many hours a contentious matter will take to resolve most divorce cases are charged on an hourly rate rather than on a fixed fee basis.

Non-contentious matters include probate, conveyancing, will drafting, etc.

As previously noted, solicitors are now obliged to supply information about their costs. This information should be given in a clear format and all legal jargon should be excluded. At the outset of the transaction your solicitor should send you a client care letter, which you are usually expected to sign and return. Your solicitor should also give you an estimate of costs up to a certain stage, and before that stage is reached, further estimates and updates on costs. It is therefore helpful if the parties agree to a cost limit, that is, a limit that should not be exceeded without further consultation. Remember however, that even though any estimates a solicitor gives should be realistic, an estimate is an estimate and is not a fixed fee.

A solicitor's work on a divorce involves:

◆ telephone calls made and received;
◆ meetings with clients and other parties;

- writing and reading documents;
- research;
- completing of forms and drafting documents;
- preparing statements.

All this work leads ultimately to preparing the case for court, instructing counsel, discussing the case with counsel and attendance at court.

The Law Society's guidelines on professional conduct state that the client should be informed as to whom is doing this work. They should be given the name of the person who is dealing with the matter on a day-to-day basis and the name of the partner who has overall responsibility for the case. This is because there are different charges for different people who are working in the firm, such as assistant solicitors, trainees legal executives, paralegals and partners. Similarly if at any stage the case is referred to someone else, the client should be informed.

Paying the bill

Your solicitor may ask you for a payment on account at the beginning of a case. When the case has been concluded the final bill should be delivered promptly. This should break down all the disbursements, or out of pocket expenses.

In contentious cases the client can ask for the bill to be taxed. This is a process whereby the court assesses the bill and either approves or reduces it. Remember that in any contentious court proceedings you are exposing yourself to the risk of paying not only your own but also the other side's costs and the final bill will reflect this.

WHO IS LIABLE FOR COSTS?

If you lose the case you may have to pay the other side's costs. There may also be costs ordered against you if you do not act reasonably throughout the case. Ultimately however it is the court that will decide the liability for the costs.

In deciding liability the court will take into account the conduct of both parties under the Civil Procedure Rules. This conduct includes:

- co-operating with the opposing party;
- disclosing and exchanging information at an early stage;
- identifying the real issues in dispute and resolving other issues out of court;
- only using litigation as a last resort;
- keeping the expense of bringing or defending a case in proportion to the issues at stake.

In bringing the action to a close the court will look at any of these, such as payment into court or offers that are made.

The court can also make the legal representatives liable for any wasted costs: a wasted costs order would arise if any of the legal representatives were found unreasonable or negligent in their actions.

PUBLIC FUNDING/LEGAL AID

There is a system for people on lower incomes to make an application for public funding or legal aid. The new Legal Services Committee Commission administers the Community Legal Service, the Community Legal Service Fund and the Criminal Defence Service.

The Community Legal Service Fund makes monies available for certain cases, including divorces. Only solicitors who are franchised or contracted to the Legal Services Commission are able to take on Community Legal Service (CLS) funded cases.

There are different types of CLS funding:

- legal help;
- help at court;
- legal representation;
- emergency legal representation;
- support funding;
- family mediation;
- approved family help.

The funding available ranges from initial advice and assistance on legal problems right the way through to full representation in legal proceedings.

Whether the applicant's funding will be accepted depends on two criteria:

1. His or her income.

2. Whether the case satisfies certain merits, e.g. the chances of the case succeeding in court justify the likely amount of funding.

3. Priority cases such as homelessness, child protection and domestic violence would also attract funding.

STATUTORY CHARGE

If the client loses the case the fund will pay the solicitor's bill, and the court will not order the client to pay his or her opponent's costs. If on the other hand the client wins the case, he or she will have to pay back the funding from any money or property he or she has recovered in the proceedings. This amount is called the statutory charge.

The statutory charge the client will have to pay is therefore based on the following.

◆ The amount the LSC has spent on funding the service less any costs recovered.

◆ Less any contribution that has been made by the client towards the costs.

The purpose of the statutory charge is to recover costs paid by the state. Certain things however are exempt, and for divorce purposes these are:

◆ maintenance payments;
◆ payments up to £3,000 in matrimonial property or settlement.

The statutory charge may be waived if it would cause great hardship or distress, or if it would be unreasonably difficult to raise because of the nature of the property.

Postponing the charge

The charge does not have to be paid immediately. The LSC might for example agree to postpone the charge subject to it being secured against the property that is being recovered, such as a freehold or leasehold property. The fund will however charge interest until the property is recovered and the money is released. The rate of interest since 2002 has been five per cent.

Conditional fee agreements (no win, no fee) are not available in matrimonial cases as a matter of public policy.

Other organisations apart from the LSC offer free legal advice, for example:

◆ The Bar – Pro Bono unit;
◆ The National Association of Citizens Advice Bureaux;
◆ Law Centres.

3

Your Property and Your Children

This chapter outlines the procedure for property, family and children.

ANCILLARY RELIEF

Applications to the court concerning property, money and children are known as **ancillary relief**. If the parties do not agree on such matters both parties may have to appear before the judge, particularly if the dispute is about children.

Only after the grounds for the divorce have been proved, and the court is happy that the arrangements for the children have been satisfied, will the *decree nisi* be granted.

The ancillary relief procedure is usually a hearing to resolve certain disputes. It is a paperwork exercise, but may involve a court hearing to resolve certain disputes. In most cases however the parties' barristers and solicitors work out a deal themselves, which is then approved by the court in the form of a consent order.

Starting the ancillary relief procedure process

Under new Civil Procedure Rules, once the application is made it cannot be stopped without the court's consent.

The ancillary relief actually starts with the filing of Form A and this is served on the respondent by the court. The pre-application protocol suggests that procedure should not be issued if matters can be agreed without an application for ancillary relief.

New rules for ancillary relief were introduced in June 2000. One of the objectives of these rules is to ensure that both parties are on an equal footing, so that the case is justly dealt with by the court. To achieve this equality the parties, as far as possible, present their evidence in the same format. Both complete a standard financial statement (Form E), which sets out the facts of the case. This document ensures all matters are addressed properly in a proportionate way.

The standard financial statement also ensures that the only way the parties can get more information is by asking the court to raise a further disclosure.

The rules also state they should be dealt with expeditiously and fairly. The document similarly sets tight time limits that cannot be altered. The courts now manage the case, and the parties are encouraged to co-operate with each other and with the conduct of the proceedings.

They are encouraged to settle their disputes through mediation and to identify the issues at an early date. Finally the extent of the documents to be disclosed is now regulated, as is the expert evidence to be called upon.

WOOLF REFORMS

Ancillary relief, like most other court actions, has a focus and timing that it did not have before, and it is now dealt with in a reasonable time in a more structured manner. The aim in most cases is not to litigate, but to settle. In making a financial order ancillary relief is a final resort. Any settlements prior to the application can result in a consent order agreed to between the parties and approved by the court.

Pre-application protocol

In his reforms Lord Woolf created a number of pre-application protocols. The idea behind all the litigation, that is any legal work items that go to court, is that as far as possible the parties should settle before making any application to court.

The protocol for ancillary relief applications is aimed to result in full disclosure and negotiation taking place at an early stage. The court will then decide that the pre-application protocol is the normal and reasonable approach that should be undertaken before any application to court is made.

If proceedings are started before the protocol has been complied with the court can make a decision, particularly concerning costs and the unreasonableness of the parties.

The protocol is designed to cover all the claims for ancillary relief and this would cover all applications for periodical payments, or a substantial lump sum and property adjustment order.

Under the Woolf reforms ancillary relief now has a court timetable and a court managed process. What this means is that when the application is made there are strict procedures and timetables laid down so that neither party can drag on the negotiations unnecessarily. Therefore there might be advantages in arranging disclosure before the proceedings have commenced, but it should also be borne in mind by solicitors that excessive disclosure in negotiations might risk running up the costs to the detriment of either party.

It is also suggested that the parties and solicitors should consider whether mediation is necessary, as an alternative to solicitor intervention or court based litigation.

Making an application for ancillary relief to the court should not be regarded as a hostile step or as a last resort: it should merely be thought of as the means of starting the court timetable, of controlling disclosure and as an endeavour to avoid a costly hearing. However ancillary relief proceedings cannot be started before the decree nisi and cannot take effect until the decree absolute.

All the ancillary relief forms should be included in the prayer, even if they are inappropriate at the time. None should be omitted. This will allow the application to be made later.

STARTING THE PROCEEDINGS

Once the petitioner (also known as the 'applicant') has decided to apply for ancillary relief he or she must complete Form A (Notice of [Intention to proceed with] an Application for Ancillary Relief). This form is then filed at the divorce court, which serves the notice on the respondent. Once the respondent has signed this notice a date is fixed for the first appointment (usually 12–16 weeks ahead). The purpose of the first appointment is to settle the case without the need for judicial assistance.

Five weeks before the first appointment the parties must exchange:

◆ A sworn statement that verifies their financial circumstances as outlined in form E (the standard financial statement).

◆ All other documents as prescribed in form E.

No less than14 days before the first appointment they must file and serve:

1. A concise statement of the issues between them.

2. A chronology.

3. Questionnaires related to the statement of issues asking for further documents or a statement that no further information is required.

No later than 14 days before the first appointment the parties must also decide whether they are going to use all or part of the first appointment as the financial dispute resolution (FDR) (see below). This is done using Form G (Notice of Response). The applicant must also confirm that every person who should be served notice of the application has been served notice.

At the first appointment the judge will give directions concerning the questionnaire and any matters such as valuations and expert witnesses.

Financial dispute resolution
There will also be directions as to the position of the case, such as the fixing of the date for the financial dispute resolution. The

financial dispute resolution is for all discussions and negotiations. The judge will see that the offer is made and this must be filed not later than seven days before the FDR. The judge may indicate what sort of settlement they have in mind.

The parties are required to use their best endeavours to settle. They must be personally present at the FDR. If an agreement is reached the court will make the final order. If no agreement is reached then the case will be sent for trial.

Offers

Offers can be made and usually an open offer is called the Calderbank offer. The Calderbank offer means 'without prejudice', but reserving the right to refer to the offer on the issue of costs.

This is usually made in writing and is the equivalent of a payment into court and is not referred to at the hearing.

If the court awards no more than what was offered the offer may then be referred to. It should protect that party on whose behalf it was sent and also the party on whose behalf it was made.

Forms

The new forms in relation to the rules are:

◆ Form A – Notice of Intention to Proceed an Application for Ancillary Relief
◆ Form B – Notice of Application under Rule 2.45 – Ancillary Relief
◆ Form C – Notice of First Appointment

- Form D – Notice of Financial Dispute Resolution Appointment
- Form E – Financial Statement – Ancillary Relief
- Form F – Notice of Allegation in proceedings for Ancillary Relief
- Form G – Notice of Response – First Appointment
- Form H – Estimate of Costs – Ancillary Relief
- Form I – Notice of Request for Periodical Payments Order at Same Rate as Order for Maintenance Pending Suit.

DISCLOSURE

Full and frank disclosure is expected in Form E and accompanying documents, which must be filed and served on the other party 35 working days before the date of the first appointment. Once the Form Es have been filed and served the parties must produce for the First Appointment:

- a concise statement of issues;
- chronology;
- a draft of any questionnaires desired to be administered;
- Form G notice as to whether that party is in a position to treat the First Appointment as a FDR appointment;
- Form H, an up-to-date statement of costs incurred so far.

PREPARATION FOR THE FIRST APPOINTMENT

Filing
The following must be filed if the process is to be commenced:

- Form A plus a copy for service;
- The fee.

There will now be a hearing date set at this stage for the first appointment, within 12–16 weeks ahead. It cannot be altered without the court's permission. Therefore most of the preparation in the case must be completed at this stage; the parties then file a Form E.

These are steps that must be completed before the first appointment:

◆ preparing Form E;
◆ exchanging Form E;
◆ completing Form G;
◆ questionnaire and list of documents;
◆ the first appointment.

The parties must file and exchange at least 14 days prior to the date fixed for the first appointment:

◆ a concise statement of the issues;
◆ chronology;
◆ any questionnaires requiring information and documents;
◆ Form G;
◆ immediately before the first appointment each party must file Form H, detailing the costs incurred to date;
◆ any questions must be authorised by the administering judge and have to be submitted prior to the first appointment. The questions have to be approved by the judge.

Preparing Form E

Form E standardises what the parties are revealing about their financial background. The parties must both file and simultaneously exchange Form E to support the application.

It is very long and detailed document, sets out all the capital, income, standard of living, and includes income, benefits in kind, outgoings, assets, pension rights, whether they intend to remarry or co-habit and any conduct which might be applicable.

The parts of the form are broken down into the following.

1. General information.
2. Financial details including property and bank accounts.
3. Securities, insurance policies and savings.
4. Cash and chattels.
5. Other realisable assets.
6. Liabilities.
7. Business assets.
8. Pensions.
9. Other assets.
10. Income.
11. Additional income – benefits etc.
12. Self employed or partnership income.
13. Investment income.
14. Any other income.

Filed along with the Form E should be:

◆ the last three payslips;
◆ the last P60;
◆ bank/building society statement of the last 12 months;
◆ any property valuation obtained in the last six months;
◆ the most recent mortgage statements;
◆ the last two years' accounts for any business or partnership plus any relevant documentation;

- valuation of any pensions;
- surrender valuations of any life insurance policies.

Part 3 requirements

1. Income needs.
2. Capital needs.
3. Significant changes in net assets.
4. Standard of living.
5. Contributions.
6. Conduct.

Conduct has no relevance in financial proceedings and should be omitted.

Financial details of the new partners

This can obviously cause some considerable problems. The simplest way is to deny all knowledge of his or her financial affairs.

Exchanging Form E

Both parties must exchange and file with the court a statement in Form E. No party should have the advantage of having read the other party's statement. Form E must be filed and exchanged within 21 days of the first appointment.

Procedure

Following the exchange of Forms E send the other side's Form E to the client and take instructions as to any further disclosure or questions.

Further action before the first appointment – preparation of:

- concise statement;
- chronology;
- questionnaire and any further information and documents requested
- a notice in Form G;
- confirmation of any other notices to be served.

Completing Form G where there is to be a financial dispute resolution

It will be correct to state that the applicant/respondent will be in a position to proceed with a financial dispute resolution appointment for the following reasons.

1. The applicant considers that the respondent has provided sufficient documentary evidence.

2. There are a number of issues as set out in the applicant's statement, which it has not been possible to resolve, upon which the applicant asks for the court's guidance.

The concise statement of issues

This would cover such things as housing, income and chattels and set out why the client has come to that view.

The chronology

This would be the history of the marriage.

Questionnaire and list of documents requested

If this form is filled in correctly it should reduce the scope for questions.

THE FIRST APPOINTMENT

Both parties must attend the first appointment unless the court orders otherwise. It is very likely that the first appointment will be treated as the financial dispute resolution so it is important that both the parties are there.

The judge's role indicates that the first appointment should be conducted with the objective of defining the issues and saving the costs. Therefore it is not necessary that the parties arrive in advance of the first appointment but it is usual for the parties to attend early with a view to settling matters.

At the first appointment the judge will decide what further documentation will be allowed at the FDR and final hearing.

The district judge decides:

- what questionnaires need to be answered;
- what documents need to be produced;
- what valuations or other expert evidence are needed;
- what other evidence is needed (e.g. schedule of assets or narrative affidavits).

The sorts of valuations that will be needed are;

- valuation of the home;
- valuation of the family business;
- any evidence of new partners' means.

The district judge will then fix a date for the FDR unless the case is:

- very complex;
- so simple that is can go direct to final hearing;
- suitable for adjournment for mediation or negotiation;
- one requiring adjournment generally.

Questionnaires and list of documents

At the first appointment the district judge must determine the extent to which any questions seeking information must be answered, and what documents must be produced. They will give directions for the production of any further documents which may be necessary.

The parties should be discouraged from asking unnecessary questions and if they do so, they may end up not being able to recover their costs.

The judge will then move on to the valuation of assets, including joint instructions to joint experts.

The judge will then fix the financial dispute resolution (FDR) hearing date.

Fixing a further directions appointment

A further directions appointment might be ordered where one party has, for example, not completed Form E satisfactorily, or failed to provide prescribed documents. It may be that out of court mediation by negotiation prior to the FDR is necessary.

Both parties need to be compliant with all the directions made at the first appointment, and all offers need to be filed not later than seven days before the FDR.

What needs to be filed are cost estimates in Form H together with the decree nisi. The FDR may not be effective without the decree nisi or a decree of judicial separation.

THE FDR

The FDR is a meeting held for the purpose of discussion and negotiation. The various parties should arrive with their solicitors and barristers, if instructed, about an hour before the time listed with a Form D notice of the FDR.

During negotiations the parties will exchange arguments and any issues between them. They will be called into the court where the commencement of the hearing and discussions of the court will follow. In the court continued negotiations over the final order and further directions will be made. If matters still have not been resolved there will be directions for trial.

Ultimately with the FDR, the judge will make a punitive costs order if a party refuses to take part in the negotiations. If matters are still not resolved there will be a preparation for a final hearing, at which all the facts will be heard. At the hearing when all the evidence has been presented and the parties cross-examined, the district judge will make an order. Consent orders can be drafted by the parties and submitted at any stage of the process for the court's approval. If no agreement is reached the district judge will take no further part in the case and will consider whether a full hearing is required.

FAMILY PROCEEDINGS RULES

Radical changes have been made to the Family Proceedings Rules (FPR), revolutionising the way in which judges will approach cost claims in ancillary relief applications.

It will still be possible to make without prejudice offers, known as Calderbank letters. But they can only ever be of any assistance at a financial dispute resolution appointment, as a trial judge will have no interest in them.

The use of open offers will become a powerful tool in the armoury of the family practitioner.

The existing principle that costs follow the event will be displaced and the general rule will be that that court will not make an order for costs either at a final or interlocutory hearing.

However, the court will be permitted to take into account the litigation conduct of a party to the proceedings. Costs will become a part of the substantive application and treated as a legitimate liability.

This liability will form part of the overall pot, and rather than pursuing its determination out to the end of the case, will be dealt with in the award.

If costs are to be dealt with as part of the substantive application, it remains to be seen what practical effect this will have on the time it will take for cases to be heard as the time estimated for trial will increase. It will also be interesting to see how practitioners will be affected by litigation conduct.

Pensions

Form P2 is the new pension form that separates the three types of pension attachment order – namely periodical payments, lump sum, and death benefits – into different boxes for clarity.

Form M1 invites parties to provide details of any other significant matters and to confirm that the pension arrangement has provided the required information. As with all forms it has been adapted to incorporate reference to civil partners. It also provides for the percentage of the pension share to be stated.

It is the view of the pensions industry and of the government that, in England and Wales, pension sharing orders must be expressed as percentages and not by using a formula method.

If it is to be disclosed as part of a voluntary process, or to shorten the court timetable, the policyholder will need to sign the form to provide authorisation for release of the information.

The date on which the pension-sharing order is to take effect is now stated as either from the date of the decree absolute or nullity, or 21 days from the date. It will be needed when a pension-sharing or pension-attachment order is contemplated. The form will need to be completed by the pension provider.

If the information is not to hand when filing Form E, there is now a requirement to produce a copy of the letter of request to the pension provider and an estimated date for production of the data.

At the first appointment the district judge can direct any party to the proceedings to complete a pension inquiry form (rule 2.61D(2)(f) Form P.

Ancillary relief scheme

There has been an Ancillary Relief Scheme since 2 June 2000. In ancillary relief matters the parties are the 'applicant' and the 'respondent'.

When applying for ancillary relief the prayer of the petition usually includes all the ancillary relief that could be applied for and if agreement isn't reached it goes to Pre-application Protocol. This covers what should be undertaken prior to any litigation and making an application for ancillary relief. Therefore ancillary relief could be obtained by negotiation between the parties without having to make any application to the court.

THE HEARING

This is usually in chambers before the district judge and will be in private. It is usually very informal. The applicant's witnesses are called, cross-examined and the various lawyers for both the respondent and applicant will address the court.

The President's Direction of 1995 set out the sorts of things that the court would require, and since 2000 Practice Directions there is a format for the content of the bundle of non-emergency cases which include:

- ◆ a summary of the background to the hearing, usually on one page;
- ◆ a statement of the issues;
- ◆ a summary of the order or directions sought by each party;
- ◆ a chronology for a final hearing;
- ◆ skeleton arguments;
- ◆ copies of all authorities relied on.

The order

The sort of things that would appear in the order are:

- Periodical payments do not necessarily run from the date of the order, but can be backdated.
- The order may be registered in the Family Proceedings Court.
- Costs can be ordered or allowed for.
- Taxation for costs for public funding if ordered.

Liberty to apply should be included to enable the parties to return to court if difficulties should subsequently arise. This is for the implementation of the order, and not for variation of the order.

Either party may appeal within 14 days of the order.

Orders sought

The kind of orders sought include:

1. Clean break.
2. Transfer of property.
3. Share portfolios and motor cars.

You will be asked for details of specific transfers, variation or dispositions, which you are asking the court to deal with.

You will need to set out if you are seeking to transfer any property or asset, and you will have to identify the asset in question.

If you are seeking a variation of a pre or postnuptial settlement you must identify the settlement.

If you are seeking an avoidance of a disposition order you must identify the property to which this applies.

Consent order under the MCA 1973, S33a

If the parties agree the court has the power to make a consent order. Application is simply made by one party or the other on Form A for an order in the agreed terms, lodging with the application two copies of the draft order, which must be signed by the respondent agreeing to the terms.

There needs to be a short statement of information called a Rule 2.61 form. This allows the court to make the order on sufficient financial information. The lawyers, not the court, draft the order and the court approves it.

Frank disclosure

It is regarded as good practice that all the parties give a full and frank disclosure. The idea is that once this has happened that there is likely to be a fairer result in the consent order.

Therefore even where there is not likely to be a contested situation then the parties should ask for the Forms E to be exchanged in draft together with tax forms. This will result in saving of time and cost if there is to be a contested case. The most amount of work in an ancillary relief case is the preparation of all the paperwork. If the parties are co-operating from the start the full disclosure may not be necessary.

4

The Law Society's Family Law Protocol

INTRODUCTION

The Law Society published a Family Law Protocol in 2002 as an attempt to create best practice in family law matters. Although specifically for solicitors it does in fact cover anyone who deals with the divorce process.

The decision was to update the Protocol regularly. The First Edition of the Family Law Protocol came out in 2002 and was issued in its second edition in 2006.

The general principles of the Protocol are as follows:

+ To ensure that all matters are resolved as speedily as possible without costs escalating unreasonably.
+ The needs of any children and family should be paramount.
+ The procedure should create minimum stress for all the parties.
+ To create a continuing relationship between the parties and any children.

There is a principle of proportionality, by which it means that the costs in the matter should not rise unnecessarily and be out of proportion to the value of the matters which are being discussed.

Part 1 of the Law Society Family Protocol covers the main protocol. The other parts cover individual areas such as children, cohabitation and domestic abuse. the whole protocol may be viewed and downloaded for free on the Law Society Website www.lawsociety.org.uk

THE LAW SOCIETY'S FAMILY LAW PROTOCOL PART 1 2006 THE MAIN PROTOCOL*

1.1 The First Meeting

1.1.1   Solicitors are reminded that the Civil Partnership Act 2004 will come [came] into force on 5 December 2005. The Act will give same sex couples the opportunity to register their relationships and thereby acquire rights and responsibilities almost entirely analogous to those of married couples. Any reference to marriage, unless the contrary is expressly stated, should be taken to refer also to civil partnership, while reference to spouse should be construed as referring also to a civil partner unless this is specifically excluded.

1.1.2   Solicitors are reminded that they must identify their clients in accordance with the requirements of the Money Laundering Regulations 2005. Clients should be asked to bring two forms of appropriate identification to the first meeting. The Law Society's guidance to the Proceeds of Crime Act 2002 and the Money laundering Regulations 2003 can be found on the Society's web site at www.lawsociety.org.uk/professional/conduct/guideonline.law as new Annex 3B.

1.1.3   In all family law matters it is important that at the first meeting or early in the case, solicitors should consider certain matters as follows.

*Copyright © The Law Society 2006.

Reconciliation

1.1.4   When instructed by clients facing family breakdown the first step (unless it is clearly inappropriate to do so) is to discuss with clients whether the relationship is over or whether there is a possibility of saving the relationship.

1.1.5   In cases where recent or serious domestic abuse or any other form of abuse is alleged, the question of whether a relationship or marriage can be saved is rarely an appropriate question to ask clients, especially if they are from backgrounds in which they have already been placed under pressure to save their marriage. It is more appropriate to inform such clients as to their rights in civil law so that they can make an informed choice.

1.1.6   Solicitors must keep an up-to-date list of referral agencies including local marriage guidance agencies, counsellors, Relate, etc and refer clients to them where appropriate. Solicitors need to bear in mind their clients' ethnic, cultural and/or religious background when considering referral agencies and should be aware of the benefits of referring clients to agencies with knowledge of their particular background.

1.1.7   The prospect of saving the relationship and /or the benefits of support groups or family, personal or relationship counselling should be kept under review throughout the case.

1.1.8   However, solicitors must consider carefully whether family support networks are beneficial where members of minority backgrounds are concerned. Many clients from minority backgrounds face acute pressures from members of their extended families to save their marriages. Wider family networks, and even the community to which they belong may add to the pressures on the clients. It is therefore important to bear in mind such difficulties when advising.

Other support services

1.1.9 Solicitors should be aware of any support services (for example debt counsellors, contact centres, Citizens Advice Bureaux, organisations for persons with addictions and/or their families). These can assist clients in coming to terms with problems which underlie their relationship breakdown, or have come about as a result of that breakdown. Solicitors should advise clients of the existence of these organisations and encourage clients to use their services when appropriate.

Interpreters

1.1.10   Where English is not a client's first language, solicitors should always consider whether an interpreter should be present throughout an interview. Solicitors should consider whether they can act for a client when they do not speak the language of the client and no interpreter is available. Solicitors should be aware that it is generally inappropriate to use family members, especially children as interpreters. This is most important in cases where domestic abuse is alleged but should be seen as a general rule. There will also be some cases in which a client may be unwilling for a member of their community to act as an interpreter and solicitors should abide by this decision.

1.1.11   Solicitors should not make assumptions about which language and dialect is required and should ensure that the services of the correct interpreter are sought. Interpreters must be independent and non-judgemental and solicitors should ensure that interpreters know that their role is limited to interpreting exactly what is said. Clients seeking advice must feel confident that their solicitor and interpreter are acting in their interests alone and that the facts of their case are confidential. It is preferable where possible to use an interpreter of the same sex as the client.

Family dispute resolution

1.1.12   If reconciliation appears to be unlikely, there are a number of ways to resolve disputes arising from family breakdown. When first instructed by clients, solicitors must:

a. Explore carefully clients' legal needs and establish exactly what clients are trying to achieve.

b. Establish whether clients' circumstances might affect the choice of a resolution procedure, for example cost or accessibility.

c. Consider the most appropriate form or forms of dispute resolution for the case or for individual parts of the case and keep them under review throughout the case. In cases where domestic abuse is alleged, the safety of the victim and any children is a prime concern and any proposed form of dispute resolution should always be viewed in the context of safety and protection. Victims of domestic abuse should not be pressurised to meet with their violent partner in an attempt to reach an agreement.

d. Consider whether, and if so how vulnerable clients and clients under a disability within the meaning of Part IX Family Proceeding Rules (FPR) 1991, SI 1991/1247 can engage in family dispute resolution.

1.1.13 The four most commonly used forms of dispute resolution in family cases are:

a. Agreement between the parties.

b. Negotiation between solicitors, including meetings between solicitors acting for each of the parties and their clients where appropriate.

c. Mediation or other forms of alternative dispute resolution (ADR).

d. Court based conciliation.

e. Adjudication by the court.

They are often used in combination.

1.1.14 Solicitors must ensure that clients are aware that in financial matters an agreement must be embodied in a consent order to be directly binding on the other party.

1.1.15 Solicitors must:

a. At an early stage unless it is clearly inappropriate to do so, explain the mediation process and advise clients on the benefits and/or limitations of mediation in their particular case, as well as the role of the solicitor in supporting the mediation process.

b. Keep the suitability of mediation under review throughout the case.

c. Encourage clients to go to mediation when and where appropriate, providing it is safe to do so.

Domestic abuse

1.1.16   Solicitors must be aware of the widespread incidence of domestic abuse and the remedies available. Information and best practice guidance (including a definition of domestic abuse, the meaning of screening, needs assessment and safety planning) is provided in Part 4. Solicitors must:

a. Treat the safety of clients and any children as a priority.

b. Screen appropriately for domestic abuse.

c. Where domestic abuse is not revealed at the first meeting, continue to keep the possibility of it under review, remembering that is can affect both men and women and can occur in all manner of family relationships and can cause harm to children who witness violence or are abused themselves.

d. When domestic abuse is disclosed, undertake a needs and risk assessment and safety planning with clients; the appropriate remedy for each client's individual needs must be discussed and kept under review. Solicitors may wish to make referrals to local domestic abuse services or advise clients of advocacy and support services available, including refuges. Solicitors should ensure that clients are aware of the crossover between domestic abuse and child protection issues. Solicitors should also be aware of the effect of the Domestic Violence, Crime and Victims Act 2004 in this area and its potential impact upon choice of remedy.

Urgent issues

1.1.17   Solicitors need to establish the basic facts of a case, establish whether there are any urgent issues in addition to those mentioned above and advise on how it is appropriate to deal with them.

1.1.18   Examples of issues that may require consideration at any early stage are:

a. The need to establish whether any without notice orders are needed.

b. The need to consider whether there is a risk that a child may be removed from England and Wales with the knowledge or consent of the client.

c. The need to establish whether there are any relevant criminal proceedings pending (in which a client may be a complainant, a witness or a defendant).

d. The need of interim maintenance to be agreed or applied for.

e. Whether maintenance for children can be agreed or whether reference to the Child Support Agency (CSA) should be made.

f. The need for clients to be advised about welfare benefits.

g. The immediate housing needs of clients and any relevant children.

h. Severance of a joint tenancy of a family house.

i. Registration of rights of occupation of a family home. Solicitors should advise clients that owners of property are now notified by the Land Registry if a matrimonial home notice of caution is placed on their property.

j. The need to make/revise wills, bearing in mind the intestacy rules, the effect of divorce on wills and the possibility of appointing testamentary guardians.

k. The need to limit access to credit cards.

l. The need to close or freeze joint accounts or to make them joint signatory accounts.

m. The need to limit draw down facilities on existing loans and mortgages which secure future loans by either party.

n. The consideration of nominations for death in service benefits.

o. The need for transfer of assets between spouses in the fiscal year of separation in order to defer capital gains tax liability.

p. The need to consider an application under the Matrimonial Causes Act 1973, s37 to prevent either the dissipation of assets or the giving of notice to quit by one of two joint names.

q. The need to consider whether a 'race' to issue a petition in a particular jurisdiction (following EU Council Regulations (EC) 2201/2003, 'the revised Brussels II') is being undertaken by the parties.

r. The need to consider immigration and asylum issues. Family lawyers should be aware that this is a complex and fast changing area of law and that immigration status can impact directly on the rights of a client in respect of their options for safety and protection. Appropriate advice should be sought from an immigration specialist if necessary.

Children

1.1.19 In any case where the parties have dependent children, solicitors should exercise particular care, even where there is no apparent dispute between the parents of the child or children. If there are child protection issues, whether arising from domestic abuse, child abduction or any other matters, the safety and welfare of the children should be treated as paramount.

1.1.20   In all children matters it is important for solicitors to bear in mind and to emphasise to clients, throughout the case, the continuing nature of the relationship of parent and child and the benefits that co-operation between the parents and recognition of each parent's continuing role brings to the children. Solicitors should emphasise to clients the importance of shielding children from criticism of the other parent.

1.1.21   When dealing with questions in respect of the upbringing of a child solicitors always need to remember that the child's welfare is the court's paramount consideration (Children Act 1989, s1 (1) as reinforced by the revised definition of harm in Adoption and Children Act 2002, S120). This amends the Children Act 1989 definition of harm to include 'impairment suffered from seeing or hearing the ill-treatment of another'. Accordingly, when acting for parents, solicitors must be prepared to advise their clients that the court will be approaching the matter from the viewpoint of what is best for the child and that this can override the wishes of either clients or children or both.

1.1.22   Solicitors should warn clients about the potentially damaging effects of involving their children in any ongoing family disputes. There are particular risks of harm to the children, in both the short and the long term, and continuing conflict, where they are encouraged to take sides or become involved in their parents' disputes.

1.1.23   The Home Office published a document in 2004 entitled *Tackling domestic violence; providing support for children who have witnessed domestic violence.* (www.homeoffice.gov.uk/rds/pdfs04/

dpr33.pdf) This gives practical advice and information on domestic abuse and children and may be of use to solicitors and clients.

1.1.24   Solicitors should make clients aware that negotiations in relation to children are separate from negotiations on other disputes that they may have with the other parent. Correspondence relating to children in particular should be separate from correspondence relating to financial and other aspects, or at least shown under separate headings. Clients should be made aware that the courts treat issues concerning children separately and independently from money issues, even if they relate to children.

1.1.25   Solicitors should use their best efforts to dissuade clients from making applications in respect of children when it is apparent that the applications are motivated by intentions other than consideration for the children's welfare. Examples are applications for contact or residence made from spite, from a wish to 'teach the other party a lesson', from a desire to track down or continue the abuse of victims of domestic abuse and their children, or from a perception that this would improve financial claims. Likewise, solicitors should attempt to dissuade parents from opposing an application for such reasons while being aware that victims of domestic abuse may have good reason for opposing contact arrangements with a violent parent that they (and sometimes their children) consider to be unsafe for the child.

1.1.26   It is recognised that the Child Support (Maintenance Assessments and Special Cases) regulations 1992, S1 1992/1815 (which provide for levels of child maintenance to be reduced by a specific proportions in the number of nights that the children are with the non-resident parent) may cause particular difficulty in contact cases. Clients should be advised that the law relating to contact is separate and distinct from child support. Clients with residence should be discouraged from applying for increased contact when the prime purpose is to affect payment of child support.

1.1.27   Solicitors should encourage clients to consider what, when and how they intend to tell their children about a parental separation and to consider doing so with the other parent where it is safe to do so. In difficult cases couples may find that mediations or counselling on this single issue can be helpful although public funding for mediation is not available unless there is a potential dispute.

1.1.28   Solicitors need to be aware that under the Adoption and Children Act 2002, S111 which came into force on 1 December 2003, unmarried fathers will obtain Parental Responsibility automatically if they have registered the birth of a child after that date jointly with the child's mother. Accordingly, where the birth has been registered after that date it will be necessary to check the full birth certificate so that the position can be established. The Act is not retrospective and thus does not apply to births registered before that date.

1.1.29   Unmarried fathers whose names are not shown on birth certificate and whose children's births were registered prior to 1 December 2003 can re-register the birth jointly with the mother and so obtain parental responsibility. However, fathers whose names are already shown on the birth certificate cannot re-register, and therefore cannot obtain parental responsibility by this method.

1.1.30 Solicitors should discuss with unmarried parents whether or not it is appropriate to enter into a parental responsibility agreement to seek a parental responsibility order, and/or make a will to appoint a testamentary guardian.

1.1.31 Solicitors should be aware of the potential benefits of a parenting plan and should consider their use from the outset. Parenting plans are available from the Department for Constitutional Affairs (DCA) on their website at www.dca.gov.uk/family/divleaf.htm or from county courts and magistrates' courts dealing with family matters, solicitors' offices, mediation services, CAFCASS office, and many voluntary organisations working directly with children. At the time of writing the parenting plan material is being revised by the Department for Education and Skills and solicitors should be alert to the availability of a new guide and planner in due course.

1.1.32 During the case relating to children, solicitors should be sensitive to suggestions from clients that a child is showing any signs of serious emotional disturbance. Solicitors should refer where appropriate to other agencies that may be able to assist, for example the child's school, GP, health visitor or any other health care professional, a counsellor or any other agency that may be able to assist. Solicitors should be in possession of the names and addresses of any local referral agencies.

1.1.33   Since 1 March 2005 solicitors must consider whether England and Wales is the habitual residence of the parties (or the child if there are child matters to be resolved) for the purposes of EU Council Regulation (EC) 2201.2003. A country might have jurisdiction on the divorce but not on children issues.

Clients under a disability

1.1.34   Solicitors must bear in mind that they cannot be retained by clients incapable of giving instructions (*The Guide to Professional Conduct of Solicitors 1999, Principe 24.04*). Incapacity includes those of a young age or those with learning disabilities, mental health problems, brain damage (including dementia) or any combination of these characteristics. A solicitor consulted by a client who cannot give instructions must identify a willing and suitable next friend or guardian ad litem to conduct any litigation (Family Proceeding Rules (FPR) 1991, SI 1991/1247, Rule 9.2). The Official Solicitor will act in the absence of anyone else willing and suitable. (Practice Note, Official Solicitor; Appointment in Family proceedings [2001] 2 FLR 155.)

1.1.35   Equally, solicitors must be alert to any information that the other party may be under a disability and in need of a next friend or guardians ad liteum. There are specific rules about service of a petition on a person under a disability (FPR 1991, Rule 9.3).

1.1.36   If a solicitor is in any doubt about whether a client (or the other party) is a patient for the purposes of FPR 1991 rule 9.1 the Official Solicitor can provide a standard medical certificate to be completed by the person's medical attendant.

1.1.37   Solicitors are reminded that when instructing an expert to advise on capacity to conduct litigation it is the solicitor's responsibility to ensure that the expert is given the appropriate guidance as to the legal test. As part of that guidance the expert's attention should be drawn to the fact that the test for capacity is issue-specific. The expert should be provided with a description of the litigation in respect of which they are being asked to assess the client's litigation capacity, including a description of the issues which the client will be expected to understand and the decisions that will be required.

1.1.38   An application to the court for the appointment of a guardian ad litem or next friend pursuant to FPR 1991, rule 9.2 should be made at the earliest possible opportunity upon receipt of medical evidence confirming the client's incapacity.

1.1.39   In the event that such medical evidence is inconclusive or the solicitor has difficulties in obtaining such medical evidence, then the matter ought to be referred to the court for directions. Solicitors should bear in mind that they may be personally liable for costs purporting to act without authority on behalf of a person under disability, whether or not that disability has been established by medical evidence (*Yonge* v *Toynbee* [1910] 1KB 215).

The initial letter of retainer
1.1.40   At the commencement of every case solicitors should send to clients a letter of retainer confirming their instructions, the extent of their retainer and any limits placed upon them by clients. They should ensure that clients verify that the letters reflect accurately the instructions given, and should normally be sent to the client following the first meeting.

1.1.41   Solicitors must warn clients of their duties under the Proceeds of Crime Act 2002 and the Money Laundering Regulations 2003, and solicitors' duties of disclosure of their clients' affairs and/or their opponents' affairs. Solicitors must be aware of the effect of the judgement in *Bowman and Fels* [2005] EWCA Civ 226 and its effect on the duty to report.

1.1.42   If at any time during the conduct of cases a client decides to ignore advice given by a solicitor, or to act in a way that the solicitor considers to be unwise or detrimental to that client's interests, the solicitor must write to the client expressing these concerns and the consequences of the action proposed by the client. In publicly funded cases solicitors should also consider costs.

Provision on information

1.1.43   At the first meeting or immediately thereafter, solicitors should consider what standard information clients might find helpful. In particular, solicitors should consider giving clients leaflets on matters relating to their particular dispute (see the Law Society's website at www.lawsociety.org.uk or Appendix 5 for details of professional ethics) or alternatively should at least make clients aware if such leaflets are available. Solicitors should also be aware that other organisations publish leaflets relevant to family matters. These include Resolution (formerly the Solicitors' Family Law Association).

Advising on outcomes

1.1.44   At the end of the first meeting or at an early stage thereafter, solicitors should outline possible outcomes to clients in writing as far as this is practicable on the information available. It is recognised that in cases where there has been little or no disclosure this outline will need to be very broad and this needs to be explained to clients. It is important that clients are not given unrealistic expectations; either of what can be achieved or of the time a matter may take to resolve.

1.2 Cost information

Introduction

1.2.1   Whether clients are privately or publicly funded, solicitors are reminded of their obligation to comply with the Solicitors' Costs Information and Client Care Code 1999 (Solicitors' Practice Rules 1990, Rule 15). A serious breach of the Code, or persistent breaches of a material nature, could be treated as professional misconduct and/or inadequate professional services. Breaches, which create prejudice for the other party or for the court, could result in cost penalties.

1.2.2 In particular, in accordance with the Code, solicitors must:

a.   Give clients the best information possible about the likely overall costs, including a breakdown between fees, VAT and disbursements (it is recognised that in family law matters such an estimate may need to be in broad terms at the commencement of a case).

b.   Discuss with clients how, when and by whom any costs are to be met and consider whether clients may be eligible for public funding.

c.   Discuss with clients, and keep in mind at all times, the principle of proportionality between the likely outcome and the probable expense of resolving the dispute, having regard also to the impact of any possible costs order.

d. Keep clients regularly updated about the level of costs.

Availability of public funding

1.2.3   Solicitors are reminded of their professional duty to consider and advise clients on the availability of public funding where clients might be entitled to such assistance. Accordingly solicitors should be aware of the levels of eligibility for public funding. Although solicitors can discuss alternative methods of funding, if clients may be eligible this should be explained to them and they must be given the opportunity of applying for public funding. The availability of public funding must be kept under review throughout the matter.

1.2.4   In discussing the availability of public funding, solicitors must explain to clients the effects of the statutory charge, the possibility of contributions, the reporting and mediation requirements of public funding and the costs protection that being publicly funded may provide in some cases. Solicitors must, however, be aware that costs protection does not apply to certificates granted and amendments made to add new proceedings to an existing certificate, on or after 25 July 2005. Solicitors therefore need to be particularly aware of the need to advise clients of the risk of an adverse order being made. Costs protection no longer applies to all proceedings under any one or more of the following:

♦ Matrimonial Causes Act 1973;
♦ Domestic Proceedings and Magistrates Courts Act 1978;

- Matrimonial and Family Proceedings Act 1985;
- Children Act 1989 parts I and II and Schedule 1;
- Family Law Act 1996 s53 and Schedule 7.

Also proceedings which arise out of family relationships under either or both of the following:

- Inheritance (Provision for Family and Dependants) Act 1975;
- Trusts of Land and Appointment of Trustees Act 1996.

1.2.5 If clients who may be eligible for public funding, whether at the outset of a case or at any time during it have consulted solicitors who do not undertake publicly funded work, they must be given the option of being referred to solicitors who do carry out publicly funded work (even if this means referring clients to another firm). If clients eligible for public funding nevertheless wish to continue to instruct their original solicitors on a privately funded basis, the availability of public funding and their decision not to apply for it should be confirmed to clients in writing.

The requirements of public funding
1.2.6   When clients are publicly funded, solicitors need to be aware of the requirements of public funding. In particular, make clients aware of the statutory charge, so as to ensure that clients are aware that there are circumstances in which solicitors' duties under publicly funded work can override their duty of client confidentiality. The solicitor is required to make a report to the Legal Services Commission, for example where there is a belief that the publicly funded client requires the case to be conducted at an unreasonable or at an unjustifiable expense to the Community Legal Service Fund or where the solicitor is simply

uncertain as to whether it would be reasonable to continue acting. A costs officer is entitled to disallow all subsequent costs following a failure report and it is important that the client should be aware of this. In client confidentiality, solicitors are referred to Regulation 4 of the Legal Services Commission (Disclosure of Information) Regulations 2000/442 (see 1B-76 in the *Legal Services Manual,* volume 1) and Principle 5.03 of the *Guide to the Professional Conduct of Solicitors* 1999.

1.2.7   Solicitors are reminded of their duty to safeguard public funds and to ensure that the funding code criteria applicable to the case remain satisfied. Solicitors must ensure that they file and serve Notice of Issue of a Certificate of Public Funding and Notice of Discharge of that Certificate.

The statutory charge under public funding
1.2.8   Solicitors should consider and discuss with the client, where appropriate, the application of the statutory charges in cases which may result in the recovery or preservation of the possession of property (for example, the protection of a right of occupation of property or the unlocking of the value of property). Such cases can give rise to the statutory charge, even where the title to the property is not in issue (*Parkes* v *Legal Aid Board* (1994) 2 FLR 850). Solicitors should remember that the charge does now apply where property is recovered or preserved for the benefit of a third party, such as a child, and may do so even where the case was funded under the legal Aid Act 1988.

1.2.9   Solicitors should be aware that the statutory charge arises where property, which was at issue, is recovered or preserved. Where the parties have been able to agree throughout on the disposition of an item of property, the charge cannot attach to it. Solicitors should endeavour to narrow the subject matter of the dispute.

1.2.10 Solicitors should consider and discuss with the client, where appropriate, the possibility of postponement of the statutory charge where property, which is to be used as the client's home is recovered or preserved – including under the Trusts of land and Appointment of Trustees Act 1996. It should be borne in mind that where the necessary conditions are met, including the payment of interest, the statutory charge over the property can be postponed until future sale and transferred onto the purchase of a new property from the proceeds indefinitely, ultimately reverting to the recipient's estate.

Costs orders

1.2.11 Solicitors must consider and explain to clients the factors which may affect the court in considering costs, including:

1. The conduct of litigation, for example material non-disclosure of documents and delay in seeking disclosure.

2. The absence of an offer or a counter-offer or an offer made too late to be effective.

3. The reasonableness of any offer or counter-offer since unreasonable offers are not helpful and will not be viewed as such by the court.

4. Solicitors should consider and discuss with the client the costs and implications of the provisions of the Family Proceedings Rules 1991 dealing with offers for settlement as set out at FPR 1991, Rule 2.69(a)–(h) inclusive. Solicitors should remember

that the specific costs implications of Rule 2.69(b) and (c) apply only in respect of 'without prejudice' offers and consideration should always therefore be given as to whether an offer should be an open one or made without prejudice. Solicitors should remember, too, that the costs implications apply, not when beating one's own offer, but when beating the offer made by the other party. The potentially heavy costs and interest penalty which may flow if the final order is more advantageous to one party than either that party's offer or the offer of the other party should also be noted.

5. In considering the implications of FPR 1991, Rule 2.69, clients should also be made aware that they could be penalised in costs, for an unreasonable failure to:

a. make a timely and effective offer;
b. respond to an offer;
c. make a counter offer.

6. Solicitors are reminded of their obligation to provide costs estimates to the court in Form H as to the total costs incurred up to the date of the relevant hearing. In preparing such estimates, they should have regard to Section 6.5 of the CPR Costs Practice Direction, which provides that the amount of an estimate is a factor which may be taken into consideration on a detailed assessment of costs by a costs officer.

Instructing counsel

1.2.13   If solicitors propose to instruct counsel in respect of any aspect of the work on the case, the costs implications of doing so must be explained to the client and authority to instruct counsel secured from the client. The following points should also be kept in mind.

1. In ancillary relief proceedings, an estimate of costs to date should be provided to counsel at all stages.

2. In private paying cases, the solicitor should ensure that he or she has appropriate security for counsel's fees, remembering the personal obligation to be responsible for payment of the fees of counsel.

3. The solicitor should remember that he or she has a duty to the client to negotiate with counsel's clerk to ensure that counsel's fees are fair and reasonable. The solicitor should seek the client's approval before concluding an agreement as to fees.

4. In publicly funded cases, solicitors should be aware that the level of counsel's fees will impact upon any costs limitation and solicitors may need to provide verification to the Legal Service Commission of the work done by counsel to support a claim for fees under the Graduated Fee Scheme.

5. Whenever counsel is to appear as an advocate on behalf of the client, the client must be aware, save in exceptional circumstances, of the identity of the barrister concerned and what arrangements are being made for the attendance by any representative of the solicitor with counsel.

1.3. Communication with the other party and with the client

1.3.1   Solicitors and parties where unrepresented must show courtesy and solicitors must be professional in all communications with other solicitors or parties. Solicitors should not give personal opinions or comments within letters. Solicitors are referred to the SFLA's *Guide to good practice on correspondence* obtainable from the Solicitors' Family Law Association 9, see Appendix 5 for contact details.

1.3.2   Communications must focus on identification of issues and their resolution. They should be clear and free of jargon. Protracted, unnecessary, hostile and inflammatory exchanges and 'trial by correspondence' upon clients and other family members should be considered so that correspondence sent by solicitors does not further inflame emotions or antagonise.

1.3.3   The impact of any correspondence upon its readers and in particular the parties must always be considered. It is crucial that solicitors or parties do not raise irrelevant issues nor unreasonably cause other parties or their own clients to adopt an entrenched, polarised or hostile position.

1.3.4   Solicitors should consider, where possible, sending any substantive items of correspondence to clients for checking initially, particularly if that correspondence contains proposals for settlement. They should send copies of all but routine letters to their clients as a matter of course, unless there is specific reason not to do so. Clients' circumstances are so varied that it would be difficult to prepare a specimen first letter to the other party. However, the tone of the initial letter is important. It should briefly address the issues and avoid protracted, clearly one-sided and unnecessary arguments or assertions. In drafting the first letter, solicitors must do the following.

- Where practicable, obtain approval from clients in advance.

- Where writing to unrepresented parties, recommend that they seek independent legal advice, and enclose a second copy of the letter to be passed to any solicitor instructed.

◆ Solicitors are warned that they should not use e-mail as a sole means of correspondence with other solicitors and of the danger of sending e-mail correspondence to a client whose spouse or partner might know and use their e-mail password. E-mail should not be used to correspond with clients unless the client has given express assurance that it is a suitable means of correspondence. Solicitors are advised to consult the Law Society's *Guidance for solicitors on the use of electronic mail* (April 2000) and *Professional ethics and IT* (June 2000). These are both available from Professional Ethics on 0870 606 2577

1.4 Giving notice of proceedings

1.4.1   Prior to the issue of proceedings of any nature, solicitors acting for applicants or petitioners should notify those acting for respondents (or respondents where unrepresented) of the intention to commence proceedings at least seven days in advance, unless there is good reason not to do so. It is bad practice for proposed respondents then to issue proceedings to pre-empt proposed petitioners issuing, unless a good reason for doing so exists. If respondents nevertheless instruct their solicitors to issue proceedings, their solicitors must warn them of the court's disapproval of such action, the possible costs implications and the impact of such action on the rest of the case (see the SFLA's *Guide to good practice on service*, obtainable from the SFLA and Appendix 5 for contact details).

1.5 Where the parties have already reached agreement

1.5.1   Separating couples may have reached an agreement on a matter prior to seeing solicitors. The agreement may have been reached in direct negotiation between the parties, in mediation or by some other method. In such circumstances solicitors should do the following.

1. Inform separating couples that they can only act for one party and that the other party should obtain independent legal advice.

2. When first instructed send to clients a letter setting out, in full, the terms of their retainer and the limits placed upon it by the client. The client should take particular care in confirming in writing any limits placed on the retainer. Any modification of the retainer at a later stage should also be notified to the client in writing.

3. Establish that the client fully understands the terms and effect of the agreement and the alternative options available.

4. Establish whether the agreement has been reached on the basis of full and frank disclosure and emphasise the dangers of incomplete disclosure (this is of particular importance in financial matters and a clear warning should be given to clients of the consequences of the making of financial orders).

5. Discuss with the client any omissions or points that need clarifying.

6. Advise the client on the implications of the agreements reached and whether it is in the client's best interest, both the short term and the long term. This includes, where appropriate, advising on other options available. In doing this solicitors need to bear in mind all the implications including the benefits attached to reaching a settlement on an amicable basis and the cost, risks and time involved in further negotiations, mediation or litigation (especially if the agreement is within the range that the court might order).

7. Solicitors should consider sending a disclaimer letter to the client for signature and return by the client in cases where the solicitor is concerned that there is inadequate disclosure or a clearly inadequate settlement. In the event that the client refuses to sign such a disclaimer letter, solicitors might consider whether this gives grounds for termination of retainer (see principle 12.12 of the *Guide to the Professional Conduct of Solicitors* (1999)).

1.5.2   If solicitors consider that duress or undue influence has been brought to bear on their clients to enter an agreement that is unreasonable or unfair, they should tell clients and advise them in writing to review the agreement. If the client refuses to do so then the solicitor should have regard to Principle 12.04 of the *Guide to the Professional Conduct of Solicitors* (1999) which says: 'a solicitor must not accept instructions which he or she suspects have been given by a client under duress or undue influence'.

1.5.3   Solicitors should advise clients on the most appropriate way to record the agreement and, as appropriate, draft and present to the court any necessary consent order or prepare any necessary agreement/documents.

1.5.4   When drafting financial consent order, solicitors should refer to the further guidance given in part IV, paras 16.1 – 16.6. Failure to advise fully and appropriately can result in negligence suits succeeding against the solicitors involved.

Criminal proceedings

1.6.1   In some cases, for example those where domestic abuse is disclosed, solicitors must be aware that criminal and civil law remedies may need to be used in conjunction with each other. Whether their client is the alleged victim or the alleged perpetrator in criminal proceedings, solicitors must be aware of the current status of those proceedings and any order made (particularly with regard to bail conditions), and consider how those proceedings might affect the civil/family proceedings and vice versa.

1.7 Human Rights

1.7.1 Solicitors must have knowledge of the Human Rights Act 1998, the Strasbourg jurisprudence and case law and must keep this knowledge up to date.

1.7.2 Solicitors should not use the Act inappropriately to bolster weak cases or to bring inappropriate points, but they must carefully consider, and keep under review, whether there is a general issue as to whether clients' human rights have been breached. If so, solicitors should discuss with clients what further action should be taken. Solicitors should consider the content of the *Practice Direction (Family Proceedings: Citation of Authorities)* [2000] 4 All ER 288.

1.8 EU and other international law

1.8.1 Solicitors must be aware that EU law affects family proceedings in England and Wales and must ensure that they remain up to date with the latest developments in the area. If solicitors do not feel comfortable with dealing with cross-border issues or EU law that is applicable in a particular case, they should consider seeking guidance from another solicitor regularly practising in this area or consider passing the matter to them to handle completely.

1.9 Resolution code

1.9.1   Solicitors must comply with the rules contained in the *Guide to the Professional Conduct of Solicitors* (1999), including the Law Society's anti discrimination Rules and the SLFA Code of Practice 9, see Appendix 2.

1.9.2   The SFLA publishes guidance notes on good practice, which are updated regularly and there is currently guidance on:

- service;
- correspondence;
- disclosure;
- acting for children;
- working the Bar;
- cases with an international element.

Copies are obtainable from the SFLA (see Appendix 5 for contact details). Solicitors should read and follow these guides.

WHAT IS RESOLUTION?

Resolution is an organisation of 5,000 lawyers and family justice professionals who believe in a constructive, non-confrontational approach to family law matters. Resolution also seeks to improve the family justice system. It provides education and training for lawyers and mediators to improve their knowledge of the law and their understanding of the emotional and practical issues of family breakdown. Resolution encourages the use of other dispute resolution methods, such as mediation and collaborative law, where appropriate.

Encouraging good practice

Resolution believes that family law disputes should be dealt with in a way designed to preserve people's dignity and to encourage agreements. The cornerstone of Resolution's membership is adherence to the code of practice, which sets out the principles of a non-confrontational approach to family law matters. The principles of the code are widely recognised and have been adopted by the Law Society as recommended good practice for all family lawyers.

The code of practice

The code of practice is designed to establish the principles of a constructive approach to family law matters. The code is not a straitjacket, but Resolution members must adhere to the code unless the law, professional rules or clear client instructions contradict it.

The code should be read in conjunction with the Resolution *Guides to good practice* and other current practice notes. (Guides are available free to members from Resolution's Office.)

General

1. This code applies to all Resolution members. You should explain to your client at an early stage the approach you adopt to family law work, what the code of practice is and provide them with a copy of the code.

2. You should encourage your clients to see the advantages of a constructive and non-confrontational approach as a way of resolving differences. You should advise, negotiate and conduct matters so as to help settle differences as quickly as possible and reach agreement. You should seek to recognise

that your clients may need time to come to terms with their new situation.

3. You should make sure that your clients understand that the best interests of any children should be put first. You should explain that where a child is involved, their attitude to other family members would affect the family as a whole and the child's relationship with his or her parents.

4. You should encourage the search for fair solutions and discourage the attitude that a family dispute is a contest in which there are 'winners' and 'losers'. You should avoid using words or phrases that suggest or cause a dispute where there is none.

5. Emotions are often intense in family disputes. You should avoid inflaming them in any way. You should not express any personal opinions on the behaviour of the other party.

6. Correspondence should be carefully considered for its potential effect on other family members. Letters should be in plain English and avoid jargon and legalistic phrases. Clients may see assertive letters as aggressive. Any communications should aim to resolve issues and settle matters, not antagonise or inflame them. Threats or ultimatums should be avoided.

7. You must stress the need for your clients to be open and honest in all aspects of the case and the consequences of not being open and honest.

Relationship with the client
8. You should always be objective and not allow your own emotions or personal opinions to influence your advice.

9. You should advise your clients on all the options available to them. Your clients should understand the consequences of any decisions they make. You cannot make decisions on your clients' behalf – that is a matter for them, taking your advice into account.

10. You must make your clients aware of the legal costs at all stages, including the risk of costs awards. You must ensure that the benefits of any step to be taken are balanced against the likely costs.

11. You should ensure that your clients are aware of other services that may help them to reach a settlement, including counselling and mediation. Where appropriate, you should explore with your clients the possibility of reconciliation.

Dealing with other solicitors

12. You should be courteous in your dealings with other solicitors and should avoid undermining the other party's solicitors in your client's or their spouse's eyes.

Dealing with a person who is not represented

13. When dealing with someone who is not represented, you should take even greater care to communicate clearly and try to avoid any technical language or legal jargon. You should strongly recommend that the other party consults a Resolution solicitor, but be sensitive to the fact that they may not be able to afford representation.

Court proceedings

14. You should consider the long-term effects on your clients and other family members of any step in the case and balance those effects against the short-term benefits.

15. If a particular step may appear hostile to the other side or is capable of being misunderstood, you should consider explaining the reasons for that step to the other side or their solicitor.

16. Before filing a petition, you should consider with your clients whether to contact the other side in advance to allow agreement on the 'facts' or particulars or to minimise misunderstandings.

17. When a Petition or Statement of Arrangements is received for approval, you must advise your client to give the other side at least seven days' notice of any intention to start their own proceedings, other than in exceptional circumstances.

18. You should discourage your clients from naming a co-respondent, unless there are very good reasons for doing so.

DISCLOSURE

In litigation matters these days there is an obligation on the parties to make full and frank disclosure on all material facts, documents and other information relevant to the issues. Solicitors are under an obligation to let their clients know of any possible breaches of this duty.

The parties should clearly identify the issues between them as soon as possible. This is why full and frank disclosure is important.

Form E is a guide as to how disclosure should be given and it contains a schedule of assets, income, liabilities and all the other material facts.

COURT PROCEDURES

It is likely that a court appearance will be necessary when the judge is not satisfied with the affidavit. When the petition is presented through the post the judge may refuse to grant the divorce. This may result in written questions or a request that the petition be amended. The petition can be re-served, that is re-issued.

The most common question might be that the grounds for unreasonable behaviour are not strong enough. The court would normally only expect up to say six incidents of unreasonable behaviour and they must be during the last six months. It would be unreasonable to rely on acts of unreasonableness going back further than that as it would then be difficult to justify that the other party has been unreasonable because you have been seen to have condoned them by carrying on the marriage.

The judge has to be convinced that the marriage has truly irretrievably broken down and that the grounds are strong enough. As a matter of practice the courts like to see that the parties have not been sleeping together say during the last six months. It would usually put that as the first ground of unreasonable behaviour as this would indicate that the marriage has broken down. Other grounds might be a selection of items such as excessive drinking, gambling, not socialising together, any incidents of violence or abuse, etc.

Sometimes the parties in an attempt to create an amicable divorce try to water down the grounds so as not to create too much conflict, but this can backfire if this then results in the judge refusing the petition.

At the moment we do not have a system of no fault divorce on demand. To obtain a result one party has to accuse the other party of some sort of unreasonable conduct. The concept is a difficult one to explain to the public as they are brought up in the belief that there must be a guilty party. The grounds are in fact irretrievable breakdown and thereafter one of the facts.

In reality it does not matter that one party has been unreasonable, as apart from very rare circumstances it does not affect the parties' properties rights.

Again this is a concept that does not find favour with the public. The public is of the opinion that if you indulge in bad behaviour this somehow affects your property rights. Logically this is a very harsh regime, but is not true. It is a harsh view of property law. As far as I am aware there is no rule that I somehow forgo my property rights if I have been unreasonable to other people.

Defended divorce

Again the current law of divorce derives from an Act in 1969 so it is over 35 years old. The public however feels that there are guilty and innocent parties. As a result they believe that a divorce can be defended. It means that obtaining a divorce becomes merely a process, which can relieve some problems and create others.

The overall ground of divorce is the irretrievable breakdown of the marriage. This means that if one party takes the view that the marriage has irretrievably broken down then it has. It becomes difficult, if not impossible, for the other party to claim that the marriage has not irretrievably broken down.

If one of the parties wishes to defend the divorce then there will be a hearing in court. Such a course is doomed to failure as some take the view that if a marriage has gone this far it has broken down. It could not be interpreted as a normal marriage to argue that point in court.

The alternative is that the other party does not claim the marriage has irretrievably broken down, but the respondent wants to cross petition; that is, to try to put forward their own grounds for the breakdown of the marriage.

Many petitioners want to accuse the other party of adultery, which may be a natural reaction if they discover they have been left for other persons. The only problem is that administratively another party has to be served with a petition and it can create more work. By going for unreasonable behaviour this results in only one petition being served and there are alternatives if they do not acknowledge the petition. Cross petitions can result in more costs but may satisfy the parties that they are not the guilty parties.

The alternative is that the parties will have to wait five years, but again this is quite rare. Unfortunately the public gain a lot of their knowledge from watching American films or the TV soap operas. In these everyone is either refused a divorce or every aspect of the divorce has to be fought out from whom is guilty to the custody of the children. It is difficult to explain and convince people that this is merely television and not real life. Only parties who can afford to defend a divorce will be able to proceed and that will only be to prove a fine legal point or for religious reasons. Parties may do it with a view to reconciliation or to prove divorce if the other party will not admit it.

Children's appointments

The statement of arrangement for children is served as part of the divorce produced with the petition. It is known as an S41 appointment if the judge is not satisfied with the arrangements. The children do not attend this appointment but both parties should do. Again this is fairly uncommon as the statement of arrangement sets out all the arrangements and unless the parties are unhappy with the arrangements then it will proceed.

Being represented in court

Most solicitors are perfectly able to resolve all matters to do with matrimonial property and children, but the clients may seek confirmation as will the solicitors from obtaining advice and assistance from counsel or a barrister to present the case. There are specialist barristers who are very good at concluding negotiations and drafting final orders.

Obviously there is a cost involved. The barrister can give the client a more independent view of the case, whereas the solicitor has been involved from the beginning and may be not so inclined to give the client the unpalatable news. The solicitor will choose the barrister and you may wish to have a conference with counsel well before the case is being heard, or at the very least on the day of the hearing. Barristers are used by solicitors for three reasons:

◆ their advocacy skills;
◆ their abilities to speak in court;
◆ their role as specialist advisers.

In the more complicated matrimonial matters and for peace of mind a good barrister is worth their fee. You will know that the case has been thoroughly presented and that you have received the best possible outcome in the circumstances.

Solicitors may also use barristers with a view to backing up their views to the client and satisfying the client that the best possible outcome has been achieved. From a solicitor's point of view it can cut down on negligence claims.

The solicitors provide all the documentary evidence and barristers are masters of getting to the point and making sure all bases have been covered. Barristers are good at what they do, as they do not want to face the wrath of the judges if there are any glaring holes in the case.

Barristers will cross examine both their clients and the solicitors as to the adequacy of the case so that it will be fairly watertight by the time the judge has read the papers or has the opportunity of asking incisive questions. Modern litigation is designed so that there are no traps or ambushes and barristers make sure that is the case.

Court etiquette

In chambers the hearings are in private and in open court you would not normally be asked or expected to address the judge directly or interrupt. You will only be expected to answer questions directed to you.

You should dress as soberly as possible. It is easy for a man to wear a jacket and tie and it would not go amiss. This is more difficult for women, but sober skirt and blouse plus jacket would be the norm.

Address the judge as sir or madam. If in doubt ask the solicitor to tell you before going in.

Even though your solicitor may ask you the questions the answers should be directed to the judge. Try not to argue with the judge, leave that to your representatives. It has to be done in a civilised manner.

What will actually happen?

The modern litigation system is mainly paperwork-based so, unlike a Perry Mason film there will not be any last minute evidence introduced. All the parties must have prior notice of any evidence.

Parties introducing matters at a late stage, or not answering legitimate questions may be penalised by a cost order against them. This is a powerful weapon to bring the parties to any agreement as the legal costs can mount up at an alarming rate.

The code requires lawyers to deal with each other in a civilised way and to encourage their clients to put their differences aside and reach fair agreements. Experience shows that agreed solutions are more likely to work in the long term than any arrangements imposed by a court. If the family has to resort to the court to resolve their dispute, it is best for all concerned that any proceedings are conducted in a constructive and realistic way to minimise conflict and distress as far as possible. The approach that any Resolution member adopts should be firm and fair. The code does not prevent solicitors from taking immediate and decisive action where necessary.

5

Pre-Marital Agreements

COHABITATION AGREEMENTS

Unmarried couples can enter into cohabitation agreements. These could govern the ownership of the property and the chattels. Because these are between unmarried parties and have an element of consideration in them they can be binding agreements, or contracts.

Pre-nuptial or pre-marital agreements previously mentioned are not currently binding, but courts can describe them as being one of the circumstances of the case under Section 25 of the Matrimonial Causes Act 1973.

All of these agreements would need to comply with the standard rules of contracts such as offer and acceptance, intention to create legal relations, certainty and consideration.

If the agreement is merely oral there would be difficulty in evidencing the agreement. If the agreement is in writing and all the above points are in existence they are enforceable.

Any agreement in connection with the issue of the home would need to be in writing because of the Law of Property (Miscellaneous Provisions) Act 1989 Section 2. It would not be enforceable unless it is properly recorded.

SEPARATION AGREEMENTS

This is an alternative to divorce. The parties can enter into a separation agreement which provides for maintenance, care for children and division of the property. They can be described as separation agreements or maintenance agreements.

If the parties agree in the separation agreement to part immediately then it would be enforceable and is not void on the grounds of public policy. This will be evidence that the marriage has broken down and is not referring to some matter in the future, which can be described as a similar term such as pre-marital or pre-nuptial agreement.

If the parties have already separated then either type of agreement can be entered into. It is essential that both parties have independent legal advice so that at any time in the future neither party can claim that they entered the agreement on the grounds of fraud, mistake, duress or undue influence.

The typical areas that are covered by separation agreements are as follows.

◆ A separation agreement in writing can form the basis of the evidence required for a divorce on the grounds of either two years' or five years' separation, which are two of the other grounds that can be used for a divorce petition.

◆ The agreement could contain provision for the maintenance of the parties or any children. This does not prevent the Child Support Agency overturning that part of the agreement. Again it does not prevent either party at some future date making an application to the court for maintenance.

◆ A property agreement could cover such matters as the mortgage, outgoings and repairs.

◆ Both parties share parental responsibility and there is no particular need to make arrangements for the children. Unmarried fathers do not automatically have parental responsibility.

The advantages of separation agreements are that they will avoid court proceedings. If they are not complied with by the parties then resource would have to be made to the courts and the usual methods of enforcement of a contract would apply.

Separation agreements are never the final solution, but like a pre-marital agreement can be regarded as persuasive. Any provision in the agreement, ousting or restricting the right of the court is void.

RIGHTS OF OCCUPATION OF THE MATRIMONIAL HOME

Since 1967 spouses have had the statutory right of occupation of the matrimonial home. Married couples have the rights of occupation, but not unmarried cohabitants. This applies regardless of which of the spouses is the legal owner. That is who is on the title deeds.

This only applies to the matrimonial home, not any other property that the couple might own. Spouses must choose which is the matrimonial home.

The courts may regulate or alter the matrimonial home rights in various ways.

- They might restrict or end those rights.
- They may take the various criteria into account, such as: the conduct of the spouse, their housing needs and their financial needs.
- The housing needs of any children.
- Any significant harm likely to be suffered by the parties.

Therefore the statutory right of occupation means that the spouses entitled to occupation may not be evicted or excluded from the dwelling house or any part thereof by the other spouse save with the leave of the court given by an order. If the spouse is not in occupation then the rights entitle the applicant spouse with the leave of the court to enter and occupy the dwelling house.

The court can even exclude the spouse who has the legal title to the property.

Matrimonial rights are an equitable interest, which is registrable against the title so it is binding on the owning spouse and third parties such as purchasers. Any registration will be actual notice to any purchaser.

Any spouse who has the right to occupation of the matrimonial home has the right to pay the rent or the mortgage directly to the landlord or mortgagee. It must be accepted. These rights last until divorce or the death of either spouse.

PROPERTY

Property is a much more difficult issue. There are two aspects to this, firstly disclosure, that is what each party say they own and whether or not that is true. Secondly what might be regarded as a fair split of the assets.

Both sides might have a completely different view. Again the courts are there to sort it out if you are in doubt. Once a consent order has been agreed and sealed by the court this is usually a full and final settlement. It is recommended that anyone who is involved in property matters takes independent advice as to values and the likely outcome of any court application. The vast majority of these are settled at the doors of the court.

From a practical point of view the drafting of the consent order can prove difficult and a precedent is set out in the Appendix. The court will amend any glaring errors and comment on the fairness of any split, but will not draft the consent order for you.

If you are relying on the other side's lawyer to draft it you may be in difficulty if you are making the application. Also you need to be sure that the consent order correctly reflects what you intended to be the outcome of the case.

The Child Support Act was originally introduced in 1991 and prior to that date consent orders had favoured lump sums to cover both the spouse and children's maintenance, normally such as the transfer of the property. Therefore there were non-resident parents who had entered into a clean break agreement prior to the CSA 1991. They now face maintenance calculations and they obviously feel aggrieved as this undermines the original settlement. The formula was revised in 1995 to take into account such transfers. The CSA has the authority to overturn such arrangements.

If the CSA has insufficient information they may make a default decision and this may result in an interim maintenance application.

Occupation orders can be made without notice on the other party. A date is then fixed for a hearing. These orders are severe and can and will only be made when it is necessary to prevent harm and restrain someone from harm. The order might also arrange for the payment of money to finance the occupation of the property by the respondent through payment of the outgoings.

There may be an order to transfer the tenancy of the property, whether public or private, to one of the joint tenants.

DOMESTIC VIOLENCE INJUNCTIONS

The law has now been consolidated and codified so that there are two forms of order related to domestic violence, being non-molestation and occupation orders. These orders can be taken out by associated persons

The Family Law Act 1996 provides relief for married, formerly married, cohabiting and formerly cohabiting heterosexual couples.

Non-molestation orders Family Law Act 1996 s.42

These orders extend protection against molestation and violence to a larger group of associated persons whereas in the past it related to only spouses and cohabitants. There is now protection for the whole family as well as those in married or unmarried heterosexual relationships. The group now includes elderly people who need to be protected from members of their family, or mothers against sons, as well as engaged or formerly engaged couples.

These orders retain harassment or pestering as well as violence. The order can be made without notice. A power of arrest can be attached and undertakings may be accepted in lieu.

Associated Persons Family Law Act 1996. s.62

The definition of associated persons covers those who are or have been married to each other or have been cohabitants or former cohabitants, who have lived in the same household, or are related, or have agreed to marry and any child of associated persons who have parental responsibility. Cohabitants are a man and a woman who are living together as husband and wife. This excludes homosexual relationships. This may change to include homosexual partners.

Relatives

These include father, mother, stepfather, stepmother, son, daughter, stepson, stepdaughter, grandfather, grandmother or granddaughter. It can also include brother sister, uncle, aunt, niece or nephew. It includes all those relationships which would have existed if the cohabitants had been married.

Obtaining a non-molestation order

An application can be made by an associated person who qualifies, or if the court decides that such an order should be made for the benefit of any party or relevant child. The application can be made during ancillary relief proceedings or on its own.

What is the definition of molestation?

The act does not define molestation, but it is regarded as being wider than violence and includes any sort of harassing or pestering.

Cases have included unwelcome calls made to the wife from whom a man was separated, behaviour induced by drugs, giving information to the papers which resulted in unwanted publicity.

The court's powers

The court must decide whether in all the circumstances, having regard to the health safety and wellbeing of the applicant or any associated person or child that the order should be made. Health is to include physical and mental health.

Without notice or ex parte orders

These orders might be made when the court thinks that there is a risk of significant harm to the applicant or a relevant child if the order is not made immediately.

The respondent might be aware of the proceedings, but is evading service and the applicant will be seriously prejudiced by the delay.

Undertakings

An undertaking may be given to the court in place of an order and this will have the same effect as an order and be enforceable as such. This is one of the most common methods of resolving a matrimonial matter. This was an established practice, but now is part of the statutory procedure.

The only difference is that a power of arrest will be not attached to an undertaking. An undertaking is a promise to do or refrain from doing something.

Power of arrest

The court has a mandatory duty to attach a power of arrest to the order unless the applicant will be adequately protected without it. The police may arrest without a warrant if they have reasonable grounds for suspicion that the order has been broken. The court may remand in custody the respondent who breaches the order.

Occupation orders

These are more difficult orders to obtain because the courts are reluctant to turn someone out of their home. Unlike the non-molestation order this depends on the matrimonial status of the parties and whether or not they have any property rights in relation to the matrimonial home. It can only be made in respect of a property, which is or was an actual or intended home and never a second or investment property.

There are three types of people who can apply:

♦ entitled persons;
♦ non-entitled persons;
♦ persons with matrimonial home rights.

The last are those who have rights of occupation which are called matrimonial home rights.

Persons who may not apply:

- a former spouse with no existing right to occupy;
- a cohabitant or former cohabitant with no existing right to occupy.

The court's powers

The court may enforce, restrict or terminate matrimonial home rights. They may prohibit, suspend or restrict the exercising by either spouse of those rights to occupy the home or part of it. The court may require either spouse to permit the other to exercise their rights of occupation, declare the applicant's rights, and require someone to leave the home or part of it and exclude the respondent from a defined area around the home.

The court may take into account the conduct of the parties and their respective housing needs, needs of any children and their respective financial resources. Also the effect of any lack of any order on the health safety or wellbeing of the parties and any relevant child and all the circumstance of the case.

Children

Most divorces where children are involved are settled satisfactorily. It is usually more difficult in the early years with young children, but after that the children can make their own decisions. The fathers may say they have been refused contact, and that by then the bond with their children has been broken irreparably. Contact orders can be entered into at any time and approved by the court.

The Children Act 1989 has become the cornerstone of the new law relating to children and divorce. Part 1 of the Act confirms that the overriding principle is that the child's welfare is paramount in both public and private law relating to children. Parental responsibility has replaced any former notions of parental rights and duties.

Part 2 changed the private law on children, by abolishing the concepts of custody, care, control and access and replacing them with power of the court to make orders. These can relate to where the child lives or as a home known as residence, and contact, that is when and how the child keeps in touch with the parent who is not resident with the child.

It also created Specific Issues or Prohibited Steps Orders.

The rest of the Act relates to public law matters defining the duties of local authorities to make such orders as emergency protection orders and child assessment orders, which assist local authorities to carry out their duties to protect the child.

Under the old law the parent who had custody was able to impose on the parent without custody a variety of decisions which could only be opposed by launching a full custody application. The parent with custody was able to make all major decisions and impose them on the other parent.

SECTION 8 ORDERS

The new orders are taken under S.8 of the Children Act 1989 and are therefore referred to as S.8 orders. The procedure behind these applications is found in the Family Proceedings Rules 1991 [FPR 1991]. The procedure creates a totally new approach to child disputes where the child has rights and the parents have duties, as do the local authorities. Normally there is a non-interventionist policy

This new approach has gone some way towards resolving child dispute problems, as it encourages better relations between parents since it is no longer necessary for either party to a divorce to insist upon custody of the children or any order at all. Joint residence is not encouraged as the children should have one home. Thus if the parties can agree between themselves there need be no orders at all.

PARENTAL RESPONSIBILITY

This is all the rights, duties, powers, responsibilities and authority which by law a parent of a child has in relation to that child and their property. The person with parental responsibility may not surrender or transfer the responsibility, but may delegate to a child's school or the local authority.

It includes such matters as providing a home and care for and control of their child. It also includes consent to medical treatment although children over 16 consent themselves. The parent has to maintain the child financially, provide education, agree to change of name, appoint a guardian.

The prohibited steps order may be made to stop the parents carrying out parental responsibility in an inappropriate way.

Who has parental responsibility?

Joint parental responsibilities reside in parents married at the time of child's birth and those who have married since. Where the parents are not married, the mother will have automatic parental responsibility. The unmarried father may obtain parental responsibility in one of five ways:

◆ entering a PR agreement with the mother;
◆ applying to the court;
◆ applying to the court for residence order and it is granted;
◆ being appointed guardian by the court;
◆ being appointed guardian by the mother or by another guardian.

If the father applies to the court for parental responsibility it is up to the court to decide whether it is in the best interests of the child to grant it.

The court will need to be convinced that the applicant is the child's father.

This will be on the civil standard of proof of evidence, that is on the balance of probabilities. Also the court will need to see commitment by the father.

The father will also need to show a degree of attachment and the reasons for applying for the order. In all cases the welfare of the child must be paramount.

Neither lack of contact nor friction between the parents is a reason for refusing a parental responsibility order. Lack of a contact order does not preclude a PR order. PR can be terminated if the father does anything which may harm the child. The lack of maintenance payments does not of itself affect PR, but it is one of the factors.

The following may acquire parental responsibilities:

* step-parents, although they do not acquire it automatically on marrying the natural parent;
* guardians;
* adopters;
* local authorities when they acquire a care order;
* anyone who has a residence order.

Parental responsibility ends when:

* a court order ends or the agreement ends;
* the child becomes 18.

Presumption of no order

The Act has the philosophy of non-intervention whereby is meant that there is a presumption that the court will not make an order where the courts decide not making an order is in the best interest of the child. It has been decided that parents are the right people to make decisions about the welfare of their children. Therefore any order that needs to be made must have positive benefits. There is also a policy of no delay.

DOMESTIC VIOLENCE

All aspects of domestic violence in family law are governed by Part 4 of the Family Law Act 1996. It has created codified law of domestic violence. The Family Law Act now has two orders which are:

◆ Non-molestation order which prohibits particular behaviour or molestation generally against the applicant or a relevant child.

◆ An occupation order which declares the existing rights in the matrimonial home or regulates its occupation for current spouses, previous spouses or cohabiting applicants.

There is now a range of associated persons who can apply for either of these orders. The association can be through family or domestic connections. This did not exist in previous legislation and creates a new set or people who can be protected by non-molestation orders (see Chapter 5).

A non-molestation order is available for any of the associated persons, but the occupation order is available for current spouses, former spouses and current or former cohabitants.

CHILD SUPPORT AGENCY

The Child Support Agency is a much maligned government agency whose job is to pursue and obtain money from the non-resident parent. The morality and logic of the system is accepted, but the agency appears to be having considerable difficulty in making the system work effectively. There was a suggestion that the government was going to introduce sanctions whereby the non-paying parent could be tagged like a criminal. There are powers to remove offenders' driving licences, but this has only been exercised five times since the regulations were created.

The Child Support Act 1991 created the CSA which started business in April 1993. In the past child maintenance was dealt with by the courts. The background was that the Treasury was going to make the absent parents pay so that the resident parent could be taken off income support.

A formula was created which calculated the maintenance payable for each child. The figures were linked to the amount payable by social services. The formulae have been dogged with problems and impossible to work out easily. The formula has been changed, but there is still a backlog of cases from the old formula and delay on the cases under the new formula.

The CSA was going to deal with all child maintenance cases, but so far it only deals with those who are in receipt of benefits. They have to use the CSA. The CSA then pursues the non-resident parent for the maintenance. So far they have had very limited success. The power of the courts to hear child maintenance payments has been taken away. Those parties who do not have to use the CSA can agree child maintenance payments in a court order and have this approved by the court.

The Child Support Agency is responsible for calculating and both collecting and enforcing the maintenance. For a fee the Agency will provide their services, but as most people who use the Child Support Agency are on benefits they are exempt from paying the fees. The Agency was formed to reduce the large amounts of income support being paid to lone parents, because the lone parents were not having much luck in obtaining payment from the non-resident parent and as a result were forced to claim state benefits.

The Act allows the Agency to treat any claim for a variety of state benefits as a claim for child support. The applicant is therefore forced to assist the Agency with the claim.

They are required to name the non-resident parent. This is of course controversial, as many mothers do not wish to name the non-resident parent, as there may be no relationship between the father and any children. Some of course may not have been aware that they were the fathers, as they had no long-term relationship with the mother. If the mother does not co-operate she will receive a reduced benefit. If she relents her full entitlement will be granted.

The mother can make an application to the effect that she will not name the father because of violence. If she genuinely believes this and the interviewing officer agrees then she will be entitled to receive her full benefit.

The government website will give you all the details of the CSA. ww.csa.gov.uk

Maintenance for You and Your Spouse

RECONCILIATION, CONCILIATION AND MEDIATION

These terms can be easily misunderstood throughout the divorce process. Reconciliation is the easiest of the three in that it merely means that the parties become reconciled, that is get back together again as a married couple and make a go of it. From all aspects this is the course of action to recommend itself. Divorce is an expensive and traumatic experience best avoided.

The system has built in at least a nod towards reconciliation, that is the parties discussing getting back together.

If you are using a solicitor they have to submit what is known as a certificate of reconciliation. This unfortunately has become just a paperwork exercise, but was originally put in the procedure with a view to at least encouraging the parties to take advice on reconciliation before proceeding with a divorce. It has now become a formality as the certificate merely declares whether or not the solicitor has discussed reconciliation.

Mediation is where the parties engage a third party who is not there to make decisions but to use their skills with a view to the parties coming to a negotiated settlement. The mediator will either meet both parties together or separately. or try to get the parties to clarify the issues. By identifying the issues and exploring the various options and helping the parties to communicate generally they will help to bring about a solution. They are not there to advise the couple concerned, but will help them examine the choices.

This is different from reconciliation, which is done with a view to saving the relationship, whereas mediation is there to resolve the outstanding issues.

This is an alternative to going to court. Formerly it was called conciliation, but this has been replaced by the word mediation which then makes it clear that it is not reconciliation.

Solicitors should consider at an early stage whether mediation is a way forward for the parties and advise that they seek it before any court action is contemplated.

JUDICIAL SEPARATION

The public think judicial separation is what is meant when they talk of separation. Separation is where the parties live apart, but they are not released from their normal marriage duties until they are divorced or have a judicial separation. It is a term that is often used, but they are very rare indeed.

The main reason they are rare is that all the same grounds for a divorce are required for a judicial separation. The judicial separation allows the parties to be released from their obligation for the petitioner to cohabit with the respondent.

It will affect inheritance in that whilst a judicial separation is in force if either of the parties to the marriage dies without a will then the estate of that person will devolve as if their spouse were dead. That is, their spouse cannot make any claim as a surviving spouse.

MAINTENANCE BEFORE THE DIVORCE

Spouses may agree a level of maintenance to be paid by one to the other during their separation. The agreement can either be a formal deed or just conform with the general laws of contract, so it can be oral.

Maintenance agreements will remain valid after the divorce unless a court order has been made.

The sort of agreements that could be included are separation deeds, but the agreement cannot oust the jurisdiction of the court to make any future orders. The courts have jurisdiction to alter maintenance agreements. The sorts of grounds which would necessitate the alteration are a change of circumstances or that the agreement does not contain proper financial arrangements in respect of the family. The court may vary or revoke any financial arrangements, or insert into it any financial arrangements for the benefit of one of the spouses or a child of the family. These powers in connection with children are only applicable where the Child Support Agency does not have jurisdiction.

A magistrates' court may only deal with unsecured periodic payments.

The other party can make an application under Section 27 of the Matrimonial Causes Act of 1973. They must be domiciled or resident in England and Wales, or have been habitually resident in England and Wales for a year before the application. The application is that the other party has failed to provide reasonable maintenance for the applicant; or has failed to make a proper contribution towards reasonable maintenance for any child of the family. The same financial considerations are taken into account as financial relief after a divorce. Application to the Magistrates' Court is under Domestic Proceedings and Magistrates Court Act 1978.

Either spouse may apply if the other has failed to provide reasonable maintenance, or make a proper contribution towards reasonable maintenance for any child of the family.

ORDERS

The orders that are available are:

◆ Periodical payments.

◆ Lump sum, not exceeding £1000.

◆ Ancillary relief, that is finances after the divorce.

◆ The orders available for the spouses are periodical payments, also known as spousal maintenance.

◆ An order for decree nisi is needed before a final order for periodical payments can be effective.

◆ The orders may contain provision for automatic increases in the future.

◆ Maintenance ceases automatically on the death or remarriage of the recipient.

◆ Co-habitation does not automatically end maintenance, but most orders are drafted to provide that this would be the case.

◆ Periodical payments may be secured on a capital asset of the payer, therefore it is subject to a charge to enable enforcement of the periodical payment in the event of it not being paid.

Lump sum orders

A decree nisi or a decree of judicial separation or nullity is needed before a lump sum order can be made. Lump sum orders are often linked to property adjustment orders for sale of property. The lump sum order may be postponed if capital might be available in the foreseeable future, such as an inheritance.

Property adjustment orders

These are not effective until decree absolute and the property can include:

◆ land;
◆ personal property;
◆ money;
◆ shares;
◆ policies;
◆ house contents;
◆ contingent assets;
◆ choses in action – that insurance policies, shares, etc;
◆ private tenancies and council tenancies;
◆ property owned absolutely or to which the spouse is entitled in reversion.

Enforcement orders

The most common methods are:

- **Warrant of execution**. The sheriff or court bailiff will visit the property of the person owing the money and remove sufficient goods to satisfy the outstanding debts together with any additional costs incurred as a result of the action.

- **Attachment of earnings**. If the person due to pay is in full-time employment the court may make an order so that the debt is deducted from their wages, by their employer, and paid direct to the court.

- **Oral examination**. A court hearing will be set where the financial situation of the person owing the money is assessed and the court will suggest how the debt is to be paid. Failing to attend the hearing can lead to a warrant being issued and the person being brought to court.

- **Charging order**. The mother's interests could be registered at the Land Registry, to prevent the property being sold without her consent. If and when the property is sold any debt outstanding will be paid from the proceeds.

- **Third party debt order**. If the father/husband is owed any money from a third party, such as a bank or building society, a court order can be obtained so that the third party pays indirectly. Alternatively any funds held in your bank or building society can be frozen.

- **Bankruptcy**. You can ask the court for a bankruptcy order. This is obviously a last resort, as the bankrupt will have to give up all their possessions of value and will have restrictions imposed on them concerning obtaining credit and carrying on a business.

Orders for sale

A court may require the sale of any property in which the parties have a beneficial interest. The order does not take effect until decree absolute is granted.

Variations are only available in fairly defined circumstances. They may be allowed special expenses to include such things as:

- care by the non-resident parent maintaining contact;
- costs attributed to long term illness or disability;
- debts incurred for the benefit of both parents or the child;
- maintenance element of boarding-school fees;
- mortgage payments on the home the non-resident parent and parent with care shared.

Pension orders

Pension sharing orders allow the court to split the pension fund at the time of the divorce with orders transferring 'sharable right in a pension'. The spouse then acquires a fund in his or her own name or by transferring the sharable rights to another pension provider.

Orders available for children

There are orders available for children to cover:

- children's welfare;
- clean breaks.

Disabled children

Where the child has a disability it is not taken into account by the agency, but the courts have power under Section 8 (8) to make an order, to supplement the maintenance calculation to meet the expenses attributable to that disability. Disabilities include:

◆ blindness;
◆ deaf or dumb;
◆ substantially or permanently handicapped by illness, injury or mental disorder;
◆ congenital deformity or such other disabilities as may be prescribed.

Maintenance agreements and consent orders

It is still up to the parents who are not claiming benefits to make arrangements for the children, outside the Agency and via the court.

Separation agreements

The parties may enter into a separation agreement, which is not a court order, but would be binding in the same way as any other contract. Since 1991 parents may still make separation agreements, but when benefit is involved it does not oust the jurisdiction of the Child Support Agency. Even if the agreement attempts to restrict the parties' rights to make any further claims the Act requires a parent who is receiving benefit to co-operate with the agency.

Consent orders

This is a way an agreement between the two parties may be turned into a court order and they can apply for a consent order. This is a court order with agreed terms by both parties. It usually has all the overall agreement between the parties covering home, maintenance, children, etc. It normally has a clean break clause and in the past the parent would forgo maintenance entirely, or accept only nominal maintenance for themself and the children in return for a capital lump sum. Because the Agency is the only party that can now make calculations concerning maintenance any attempt by the consent order to exclude the Agency would not now be possible.

CALCULATING THE CHILD MAINTENANCE

When the Child Support Agency is involved a formula is applied in order to calculate the maintenance payable in respect of the child by the non-resident parent.

The pre-CPSSA Formula 2000

This was very complicated and was revised annually to come in line with income support. The new formula is simpler and is based solely on the non-resident parent's income net of tax and national insurance, pension payments and the number of children for whom that parent is responsible.

The rates are called the basic rates, the reduced rate, the flat rate and the nil rates.

Shared care

Where there is shared care the maintenance contributions will be reduced. This will be dependent on the number of qualifying children and the amount of time they spend in the care of each parent.

Interim orders

These are:

+ Maintenance pending suits;

- Interim lump payments/property adjustment orders;
- Variation of orders.

Maintenance during divorce proceedings

As the main financial settlement of a divorce is not made until the decree nisi and does not apply until the decree absolute, the court will allow you to claim what is known as a maintenance pending suit (MPS).

These are periodical payments, which are either made to the petitioner or the respondent under Section 22 of the Matrimonial Causes Act 1973 as amended by the Family Law Act 1996 while the divorce is going on.

MPS can be sought at any time after presentation of the petition. However this needs to be done as soon as possible as it may take several weeks for the judge to consider the application and grant any order. However the order can be backdated to when the petition was filed.

To obtain an MPS order:

- Obtain an application form from the court office.

- Also from the court office obtain an affidavit form, on which you must specify your means supported by pay slips, etc.

- The district judge at the directions hearing will issue directions about the evidence required.

- The other side has to be served with an application and must swear the affidavit declaring their means and needs.

♦ Payments can be made either weekly or monthly.

How to enforce the payment of maintenance

What happens if your maintenance payments are not made? There are various methods of enforcing maintenance payments through the county court. You can also make a claim through the magistrates' court, unless it was originally set up in the county court.

You take a copy of the original order for the county court. The court will then become the recipient of the payment and once the court receives the money they will pay it to you.

If you make a complaint to the court, or if the payments are in arrears, the court will have a hearing to investigate the means of the person who should be paying.

⑧

Civil Partnerships

CIVIL PARTNERSHIP ACT 2004

The Family Proceedings (Amendment No 5) Rules 2005 (SI 2005/
2922) have amended the Family Proceedings Rules 1991 (SI 1991/
1247) and implemented the Civil Partnership Act 2004 (CPA).
This received royal assent on 18 November 2004 and came into
force on 5 December 2005. Rules 75 to 90 and 117 (a) 9 vii), (u),
(y) to (bb) and 120 came into force on 30 December 2005.

The Act allows same-sex couples to register their partnership, so
that every right and responsibility arising from marriage between
heterosexuals is available to them, apart from a religious
ceremony.

To register a civil partnership the parties must not be of the
opposite sex, already a civil partner or legally married, younger
than 16 years of age and within prohibited degrees of relationship
(for example, a child, adoptive child, parent or sibling).

These rules brought other significant changes to the ancillary
relief brought in or after December 2005. The filing of Form A
constitutes commencement of financial proceedings.

The rules and new forms can be found of the website of the Office
of Public Sector (www.opsi.gov.uk).

Termination of a civil partnership may give rise to a financial claim, and all claims will be commenced in accordance with the existing ancillary relief procedure. Form E has undergone a radical change to enable claims under the Act. It has also been changed to ensure that more detailed information is supplied on pension provision, property and business assets.

The requirement to provide detailed pension information has been reduced. Now only basic information is required. This includes:

- type of scheme;
- cash equivalent transfer value;
- whether payment is needed.

REGISTRATION

A civil partnership is formed when two people have signed a partnership document in the presence of each other, the registrar and two witnesses. The registration must take place in England and Wales and may not be in religious premises.

Each of the proposed civil partners must give notice of the proposed partnership to their local registration authority (section 5 (1) of the CPA). They may choose in which authority they wish to register their partnership. However they must both have resided, that is to say, have been physically present, in England and Wales and in an authority area for at least seven days prior to giving notice of the intended registration.

If a party or persons are subject to immigration controls then, for the purposes of entering into the partnership agreements, they must either obtain entry clearance, or obtain it from the home secretary, or fall within a class of persons specified by the secretary of state. Reporting duties will fall on any authorised person who suspects the formation of the partnership is for the sole purpose of evading statutory immigration controls.

When notice is given the authority will require evidence of name and surname, age, any form of civil partnerships or marriage, and proof of their nationality, and the requisite residence in England and Wales for the seven days preceding the giving of notice.

After giving notice the parties must wait a further 15 days (save where the registrar-general is satisfied there are compelling reasons for shortening the period). Notice must be publicised by the authorities for 15 days in both the authority areas where the parties live, if different. During the 15-day waiting period any person may object to the proposed partnership.

At the conclusion of the waiting period the registrar is under a duty at the request of one or both civil partners to issue a partnership schedule (except where an objection has been recorded or where the authority believes there may be a lawful impediment). The proposed civil partners have 12 months from the date of the first civil partner's notice to sign the schedule. Once the proposed civil partners have signed the schedule, a partnership will have been formed.

TERMINATION, ANNULMENT AND DISSOLUTION

Civil partnerships will be brought to an end on the occurrences of the following events:

◆ Death.

◆ Presumption of death – orders can be made by the court where there are reasonable grounds for supposing the other civil partner is dead.

◆ The fact a civil partner has been absent for a period of more than seven years, and the applicant has no reason to believe that the partner has been living within that time, will be sufficient time to assume that the civil partner is dead.

A partnership will be declared a nullity if there is a procedural irregularity of which both parties were aware at the time of registration, or if the parties were not eligible to register as civil partners.

Procedural irregularities will include failure to give proper notice, a partnership document not being issued, place of registration being incorrectly specified in the notice, and a registrar not being present (section 49). In these instances the partnership will be considered void ab initio and can only be validated at a later date by an order of the Lord Chancellor in limited circumstances.

A civil partnership is voidable where:

◆ parties do not validly consent;

◆ either party was suffering from a mental disorder as to be unfit for partnership;

◆ one party was pregnant by another person other than the other party;

- after formation an interim gender recognition certificate has been issued;

- one party has acquired gender under section 50 of the Gender Recognition Act 2004.

There is no requirement to consummate a partnership or for the relationship to be sexual.

Proceedings for nullity must be commenced within three years of the formation of the partnership.

The ground for dissolution is 'irretrievable breakdown' of the partners' relationship proved by the existence of any of the four facts that mirror section 1(2)(b)-(e) of the Matrimonial Causes Act 1973 (MCA).

Adultery is not a fact, that is, not a ground for dissolution. However, sexual infidelity may fall within the grounds of unreasonable behaviour.

A dissolution order would not be granted under paragraph (c) (separation for five years) if it would cause grave financial hardship to the respondent and it would be wrong in all the circumstances to dissolve the partnership.

As with a divorce, no application may be made for a dissolution order before a year has elapsed from the date of the formation of a partnership. However, the time bar does not prevent an application being made on the basis of events that occurred during that first year (section 41).

FINANCIAL CLAIMS

Section 72 makes provisions for financial relief for civil partners. Sub section (1) states that schedule 5, containing the ancillary relief provisions, corresponds to provisions made for financial relief in connection with marriages under the Matrimonial Causes Act 1973.

Schedule 5 sets out the orders available as follows.

- Periodical payments to a civil partners or to any person for the benefit of a child of the family or to a child of the family (any such order may be secured).
- Property adjustment.
- Variation of settlement.
- Sales of property.
- Pension sharing.

On a par with the MCA, there are several factors that the court will take into account when it exercises its jurisdiction in relation to financial orders made on the termination of a civil partnership.

It must take into account all the circumstances of the case, giving first consideration to the welfare of any child of the family who is younger than 18 years of age (schedule 5, paragraph 20).

Schedule 5 paragraph 21 (2) almost identically mirrors the factors set out in section 25 of the Matrimonial Causes Act 1973. The court, when deciding whether or not to exercise any of its powers under section 72, will be likely to adopt the approach taken in interpretation of the section 25 criteria. Only time will tell how the courts will approach the distribution of assets. However, it is anticipated that cases such as *White* v *White* [2000] 2 FLR 981 will be followed.

It is reasonable to expect that the length of the partnership, and any pre-agreement co-habitation, will be dealt with in line with the findings in *GW* v *RW* [2003] 2 FLR 108 and *CO* v *CO* (ancillary relief: pre-marriage cohabitation) [2004] 1 FLR 1095.

The cases of *Miller* v *Miller* [2005] EWCA civ 984 and *McFarlane* v *McFarlane* [2004] EWCA civ 872 will be heard together on appeal to the House of Lords and, doubtless, those decisions will apply in appropriate cases.

Many same sex couples will have lived together for a long time, and the registration of their partnerships will be a binding acknowledgement of enduring relationships.

Pre-registration agreements

What then of any attempt to enter into a binding pre-registration agreement? This is the equivalent of a pre-marital agreement. In *K* v *K* (ancillary relief; pre-nuptial agreement [2003] 1 FLR 120 and *M* v *M* (pre-nuptial agreement [2002] 1 FLR 654, we have seen a willingness by the court to uphold any such agreements entered into by civil partners.

The civil partnership is born entirely out of statute. Marriage, by contrast, has its roots in canon law and was intended to be a union for life. No such expectation is placed, statutorily, on civil partners. Why then should agreements properly entered into by civil partners to provide for the distribution of assets on dissolution of their agreement be seen to offend judicial or public policy? In cases where the court does not have to concern itself with provision for children, there may be a greater willingness to uphold pre-registration agreements.

9

Happily Ever After?

MAKING A WILL

Although this book is about divorce one of the consequences of divorce is that the rules on inheritance are changed. That is, if either married party died without a will or intestate then the other might have some automatic rights under that intestacy.

Once the parties are divorced they revert to their single person status and most people would not want the laws of intestacy to rule their estate. You are therefore strongly advised to make a will. Marriage and divorce are two of the statutory instances where a will is automatically revoked. This means on the pronouncement of the decree absolute that any former will is not now valid.

Anyone over the age of 18 who has property needs to leave clear instructions as to how their estate should be distributed on their death. Also by executing a valid will you can choose to whom your estate will be distributed; there is a fairly liberal regime in England and Wales as to whom you might leave your estate. The only statutory exception is that you must make reasonable provisions for any family or dependant that you are currently maintaining. The requirements as to who might make a valid will are as follows:

♦ must be over the age of 18;
♦ must have full mental capacity.

There are limited exceptions to the above, but they are the basics. As mentioned the main reason to make a will is to ensure that you leave your estate to those whom you wish to benefit. If no will is made the statutory rules of intestacy take place and broadly they are as follows.

- Spouses that is husband or wife, which of course after a divorce no longer applies.
- Children including all natural children and those who are adopted.
- Parents.
- Brothers and sisters.
- Half-brothers and sisters.
- Grandparents.
- Uncles and aunts.
- Uncles and aunts of half-blood.

Ultimately the state will be able to take your estate if there is no one in the above categories who can be found. Therefore some people take the view that, for no other reasons than to deprive the Chancellor of the Exchequer, everyone must make a will.

If there are no children and the deceased's parents are still alive it will revert to them. The right of a spouse ceases as soon as the divorce is pronounced.

PROVISIONS OF A WILL

The main purpose of a will is to give to your executors, the people you have appointed to carry out the terms of your will, instructions as to what should happen to your estate after death.

Subject to the rules on cutting out a member of your immediate family or those who you support you have complete testamentary freedom. Subject to the payment of your funeral and testamentary expenses, including any inheritance and income tax you may owe, you may leave everything to the cats' home if you wish.

Wills can be straightforward or complicated. A will should be easily understandable by those left behind. If they become too clever they will create uncertainty and your wishes may not be carried out. A simple test is that you should be able to read it once and understand it.

COHABITATION

Generally a cohabitant or common law wife or husband cannot claim. There is a common misconception that a common law relationship bestows some sort of property or maintenance rights. The law is changing, but at the moment there is no automatic right. The Family and Dependants Act 1975 allows a claim by a cohabitant who was being maintained, but this falls well short of a full 50/50 split which may be available under a divorce settlement.

Some testators make detailed lists of where all their assets should be given to. It is easier to divide them into financial or pecuniary legacies, that is, sums of money or specific legacies of actual physical things.

If something is of sentimental value it could be given away during a person's lifetime. Other actual physical things that may have value to you may not have the same value to the recipient unless it can be turned into money. It may become a burden rather than a godsend. Again generally all the beneficiaries are interested in is money.

A straightforward will for a divorced person with children would cover the following.

♦ Revoke all previous wills.
♦ Appoint executors.
♦ Appoint guardians for the children whilst they are under the age of 18, as a minor cannot give a valid receipt for money.
♦ A list of both specific and pecuniary legacies.
♦ Where the residuary estate would go after payment of debts, usually to the children equally and thereafter to their children in the event of their predeceasing the testator.

This would have the effect of creating a will that would not have to be changed in the short term.

A common question is 'Can the executors be beneficiaries?' The answer is yes. The only party who may not inherit under a will is a witness.

Wills have to be executed in a strict manner, so make sure the witnesses are not beneficiaries and are not related to the beneficiaries in any way such as husband or wife.

If the children are of age they can be the executors of their parent's will and also beneficiaries.

It is highly recommended that a will be prepared professionally for no other reason than if there is an error then the beneficiaries will have some recourse if the will writer has been negligent. If you make a home-made will and it has not been correctly drawn then the beneficiaries will inherit the problem, which by that time is irresolvable. Professionals are not immune from mistakes, but they are insured. Paying a lawyer's bill on this occasion will at least give you peace of mind.

TERMINOLOGY

Home-made wills can be a minefield of problems and some of the following words need to be understood.

Executor/executrix

These are the people you appointed to carry out the terms of your will. Their duties are to have the estate valued, collect in any assets, pay any debts including inheritance tax and distribute the estate in accordance with the terms of the will.

You can appoint individuals, firms of solicitors or banks to carry out these functions. As stated previously they can be beneficiaries under the will if they are individuals. If they are organisations they can only charge for their services if there is a specific remuneration clause in the will.

From a practical point of view it is better to have more than one executor and maybe some alternatives in the event of certain people not being able to carry out the functions. Therefore include more than one generation to cover all eventualities.

Beneficiaries

A beneficiary is anyone who obtains some benefits under the will. Both legitimate and illegitimate children are included.

Trustee

This is the term which can most confuse the public; they have a specific view as to what a trust is. The most common form of trust is when the beneficiary is under the age of 18 and therefore cannot give a valid receipt.

The trustee, who is usually also the executor, holds the money or property in trust until the beneficiary comes of age. An age other than 18 can be specified. The trustee is the legal owner and the beneficiary is the beneficial owner. This means that the trustee must transfer the legal title when the trust ends, usually by sending a cheque. Evidence of title comes from the will and the grant of probate.

Wife and husband

Both of these refer to the wife or husband at the time of making the will. Therefore a divorce can make the will invalid. A will can be made in anticipation of marriage and the wife or husband can be named, i.e. someone making a will before honeymooning abroad would be an exception to the rules that marriage revokes a will.

Safekeeping

At the time of writing there is no centralised register of wills that is easily searchable. Your will should be kept in a safe place, preferably with your lawyer, and your executors should be informed as to where it is being held.

PROBATE

Probate means that where there is a will executors' powers are confirmed by the court by the issue of a grant of probate. In the event of there being no will it is known as administration. The administrators gain their powers, which are confirmed by a grant of probate or of administration, given by the court.

The actual grant of probate is a document, produced by the court naming the deceased, the date of death and the executors. An official copy is issued and office copies which are impressed with the court seal are used by the executors to prove their powers and are used to collect in the assets and transfer property.

These documents are public documents and, like a will once it has been proved, copies can be obtained from the Probate Registry. The original has a copy of the will bound within it.

Small estates

If the estate is very small, say under £5,000, probate may not be needed.

Applying for probate

Where there is a will the executors apply for probate, but in the event of intestacy someone can become the administrator. There is an order of priority of who can be an administrator. It is similar to the rules of intestacy, as follows.

* surviving spouse;
* child of the deceased;
* parent of the deceased;
* brother or sister of the deceased;
* another relative of the deceased.

Applications for probate can be made through any probate registry or office. It can be made personally without the use of a lawyer.

CHANGE OF NAME

In England and Wales an adult can use whatever surname he or she chooses to use. Therefore anyone can choose to adopt a new surname, provided that this is not done with fraudulent intent. A married woman need not take her husband's surname and many women are choosing to keep their maiden name.

From the point of view of the law anyone can change their name as and when they decide to do so. There are however people such as banks who may not be prepared to accept such an informal change and they will need formal proof of the name change. On marriage, generally a copy of the marriage certificate will be accepted as sufficient evidence, but otherwise the person may need to produce one of the three following documents.

- A note signed by a respected member of the community (e.g. doctor, JP, clergyman).

- A statutory declaration. This is an official way of formalising the change of name. It is a sworn statement and a solicitor would normally prepare this.

- Deed poll. This is the most formal method and is most commonly used.

INHERITANCE (PROVISION FOR FAMILY AND DEPENDANTS) ACT 1975

This is the exception to the rule that you have complete testamentary freedom. Certain categories of family and dependants can make a claim against your estate if they are inadequately provided for in the event of your death, whether there was a will made or not. A spouse can be awarded whatever the court thinks reasonable. The same sort of principles would apply as if there had been a divorce. The categories that can claim under the will are these.

♦ Wife or husband of the deceased.
♦ Any former wife or husband of the deceased who has not remarried.
♦ Any child of the deceased.
♦ Any person who was treated as a child of the deceased.
♦ Any other person who was being maintained by the deceased prior to the death.

Dependants

This can cover a wide range of applicants, but maintenance only is payable, not a lump sum.

10

Statutory Background to Divorce

This chapter lists the main Acts of Parliament that affect divorce law.

MARRIED WOMEN'S PROPERTY ACT 1882

This act looks *back* to how property rights arose. It is purely procedural and declaratory and gives effect to existing rights. It considers conduct irrelevant and children's interest generally are irrelevant.

LAW OF PROPERTY ACT 1925

An act to make new provision with respect to deeds and their execution and contracts for the sale or other disposition of interests in land; and to abolish the rule of law known as the rule in Bain *v* Fothergill.

MATRIMONIAL CAUSES ACT 1973

This is the main act that covers the breakdown of marriage and the grounds for divorce. S23 financial provision orders in connection with divorce proceedings, etc. set out the orders that may be made. The most important section is about the powers under sections 23, 24 and 24a the court shall take, in particular having regard to the following matters.

♦ The income, earning capacity, property and other financial resources which each of the parties of the marriage has or is likely to have in the foreseeable future, including in the case of earning capacity any increase in that capacity which it would, in the opinion of the court, be reasonable to expect a party to the marriage to take steps to acquire.

♦ The financial needs, obligations and responsibilities which each of the parties to the marriage has or is likely to have in the foreseeable future.

♦ The standard of living enjoyed by the family before the breakdown of the marriage.

♦ The age of each party of the marriage and the duration of the marriage.

♦ Any physical or mental disability of each of the parties to the marriage.

♦ The contributions which each of the parties has made or is likely to make by looking after the home or caring for the family.

♦ The conduct of each of the parties, if that conduct is such that it would in the opinion of the court be inequitable to disregard it.

♦ In the case of proceedings for divorce or nullity of marriage, the value to each of the parties to the marriage of any benefit which, by reason of the dissolution or annulment of the marriage, that party will lose the chance of acquiring.

INHERITANCE (PROVISION FOR FAMILY AND DEPENDANTS) ACT 1975

This is the act which restricts your total freedom to leave your estate to whom you like and application for financial provision from the deceased's estate may be made.

It applies where someone dies domiciled in England Wales and is survived by any of the following.

◆ The wife or husband of the deceased.

◆ A former wife or former husband of the deceased who has not remarried.

◆ A child of the deceased.

◆ Any person who in the case of any marriage to which the deceased was at the time a part was treated by the deceased as a child of the family in relation to that marriage.

◆ Any person who immediately before the death of the deceased was being maintained, either wholly or partly by the deceased.

That person may apply to the court for an order under Section 2 of this act on the ground that the disposition of the deceased's estate affects his will, or the law relating to intestacy or the combination of his will and that law, is not such as to make reasonable financial provision of that applicant.

Cohabitees

Since 1996 any person who during the whole of the period of two years ending immediately before the date the deceased the person was living in the same household as the deceased and as the husband or wife of the deceased may also make a claim.

Reasonable financial provisions

This means such financial provision as it would be reasonable in all the circumstances for the case of the applicant to receive for their maintenance.

Maintenance means that the deceased, otherwise than as part of a contract, was making a substantial contribution in money or money's worth toward the reasonable needs of that person.

The court has powers to make orders concerning the distribution of the estate.

DOMESTIC VIOLENCE AND MATRIMONIAL PROCEEDINGS ACT 1978

Either party to a marriage may apply to a magistrates' court for an order on the ground that the other party to the marriage has:

a) failed to provide reasonable maintenance for the applicant; or

b) failed to provide, or to make a proper contribution towards, reasonable maintenance for any child of the family; or

c) behaved in such a way that the applicant cannot reasonably be expected to live with the respondent; or

d) deserted the applicant.

The powers that the court has to make orders for financial provision include periodical payments, lump sums and an order for the benefit of the child.

CHILD ABDUCTION ACT 1984

It is an offence for anyone to take or send a child out of the United Kingdom without the appropriate consent.

CHILDREN ACT 1989

The courts will determine the welfare of the child. This includes the upbringing of the child and administration of the child's property or any income arising from it. The child's welfare should be the court's paramount consideration.

The act covers parental responsibility for children and defines parental responsibility. This means all the rights, duties, powers, responsibilities and authority which, by law a parent of a child has in relation to the child and their property.

The act sets out how parental responsibility may be acquired by the father in the situation where the father and mother were not married.

An application may be made to the court in respect of the child, and to appoint an individual to be the child's guardian.

The act defines residential contact and other orders in respect of children.

CHILD SUPPORT ACT 1991

This defines a duty to maintain and for the purposes of this act a parent of a qualifying child is responsible for maintaining him or her.

The purpose of the act is that an absent parent shall be taken to have met their responsibility to maintain any qualifying child of theirs by making periodical payments of maintenance with respect to the child of such amount, and at such intervals, as may be determined in accordance with the provisions of the act.

The act defines the welfare of the children in general principles and sets out a calculation of maintenance.

FAMILY LAW ACT 1996

This sets out the rights concerning the matrimonial home whereby one spouse has no estate.

One spouse is entitled to occupy a dwelling house by virtue of a beneficial estate or interest or contract and the other spouse is not so entitled. The spouse not so entitled has the following rights as the matrimonial home rights. If in occupation, there is a right not to be evicted or excluded from the dwelling house or any part of it by the other spouse except by leave of the court, and if not in occupation a right with the leave of the court so given to enter into and occupy the dwelling house.

Frequently Asked Questions

What do I do if my marriage is breaking down?
Many couples may seek the advice of a mediation service. This is where the couple might meet to resolve any issues that have arisen concerning the breakdown of the marriage.

It can take place in a solicitors' practice but there are organisations that are involved in this.

What alternatives have I got to a divorce?
The parties could agree to a reconciliation or a separation. Separation could either be a form of separation with an agreement to cover financial matters and children, or an informal separation. A written agreement is a binding contract between the parties.

Judicial separation is a fairly rare application, as all the grounds for divorce need to be approved. What it does allow the court to do is to make orders about property and children.

I have been through all the preliminaries, how do I start a divorce?
To start a divorce in England and Wales, for a marriage to be dissolved, the parties need to be domiciled at least one year before the application and it must be at least one year after the marriage.

What sort of grounds do I need?
The overall evidence is to be the irretrevable breakdown of the marriage, but it has to be one of five facts, these being:

- adultery;
- unreasonable behaviour;
- desertion;
- two years' separation;
- five years' separation.

How long will it take?

Divorce will take on average between four to six months, but this will not cover financial and matters concerning the children, as they have a separate timetable.

What is the first stage of divorce

The first stage is decree nisi. If the court is satisfied that the grounds for divorce have been approved the divorce is not final until a decree absolute, which is some six weeks thereafter.

What happens about our assets?

The matrimonial home is the most important; people need places to live. If the property is in joint names it can then be sold by both parties. If it is in one of the married parties' names the other party can be protected by registering at the Land Registry. In the case of unmarried parties the matter relies on the title deeds and can be more difficult.

Who is responsible for bank accounts and liabilities?

The parties are jointly responsible for the accounts which are in their joint names.

What sort of financial settlements could I expect to receive?

A clean break is where the parties agree while ordered that neither party will claim maintenance or claim from each other in the future, and the courts encourage the parties to become financially independent with a clean break settlement.

Maintenance can be ordered, but this will end if the parties remarry.

What sort of maintenance can the children expect to receive?
Maintenance is usually payable to children until they reach the age of 17 or cease full-time education, whichever is the later.

The parties are always responsible for maintenance for their children and this is now governed by the Child Support Act 1995.

What happens to the pensions?
It is possible to drive pensions through a pension sharing law order. This will enable the wife to transfer money out of her husband's pension scheme and start a scheme of her own.

Do the current earnings of my new wife or cohabitant have any effect?
This will take effect until remarriage or cohabiting with a new partner who supports her. If the spouse's or cohabitant's income are taken into account it is their ability to look after themselves in the future.

What sort of orders can we get now for children?
The four main orders are:

- Residence, which was previously custody, which states where the child is to live.
- Contact, previously access, this allows the child to stay with a named person.
- Prohibited steps, this prohibits specific steps in relation to a child such as change of surname.
- Specific issue, this is relating to the child such as education, ill treatment.

Glossary

Abduction of child Taking the child away by force.

Abortion Termination of a pregnancy.

Absent parent The parent with whom the child is not living.

Access The ability to contact the child or the right to contact the child.

Acknowledgement of service When the defendant agrees that the document has been served upon them and has been received. The defendant signs a document called Acknowledgement of Service to confirm in writing that the documents were received.

Adoption The legal process whereby non natural parents become legal parents of a child.

Adultery Consensual sexual intercourse between a man and a woman, one who of whom must be married.

Affidavit A written statement which is sworn by the originator of the affidavit to confirm that it is true, usually sworn in front of a solicitor or the court.

Ancillary relief The financial applications that can be made to the court to cover both property and income.

Appeal Asking the court to overturn a lower court's decision, an appeal is lodged to take it to a higher court.

Arrest, power of A right to seize someone so that they are taken into custody.

Assets Property such as land, buildings, money.

Bailiffs The persons authorised by the court to take goods and sell them to satisfy a debt. They can also serve, that is deliver, documents on people.

Bankruptcy An order made by the court concerning someone who cannot pay their debts. Their assets may be sold. A trustee in bankruptcy may be appointed who takes over that person's financial affairs.

Behaviour Unreasonable behaviour in the matrimonial sense.

Benefits Agency Government department which administers and pays out benefits.

Calderbank letter A letter that is used by the parties to try to settle by way of offers which are not then known to the judge. If ultimately any of the parties gets less than they were offered after a Calderbank letter they may end up paying costs from the date of the letter.

Care order An order made by the court giving the local authority the right to care for a child.

Chambers The judge's private office, not in open court.

Chattels Any property other than freehold land.

Child Benefit Benefit paid by the Benefits Agency in respect of children.

Child of the family A technical term that means a child being treated as a member of the family.

Child Support Act This act deals with the Child Support Agency.

Child Support Agency The government body now charged with dealing with maintenance payments for children.

Civil litigation Any matter that is not a crime is a civil matter and goes through the civil courts, such as the county court.

Clean break Usually by way of a court order or consent order whereby the parties settle all their financial difficulties or matters in one go.

Cohabitation Living together without being married.

Conciliation A court-based process trying to make the parties agree differences, usually about arrangements for children.

Consent Agreement by the parties such as consent order.

Consortium The right of a married couple to live together.

Contact order The right of the various parties to make an application to the court to see the children.

Contempt of court Disobeying a court order, disrupting a court case or interfering with the administration of justice.

Co-respondent The other party in an adultery petition.

Costs Solicitors call their bills costs and you may end up paying the other side's costs if you do not comply with the court procedure.

County court Part of the civil court system, deals with divorces, etc.

Damages In the civil system damages are a financial penalty.

Decree absolute The final decree which ends the marriage. It will affect inheritance rights.

Decree nisi The decree of a divorce. You may apply for a decree absolute six weeks later.

Desertion Leaving a party to a marriage without their consent.

Directions Suggestions by the court as to how the case may proceed, such as timing and reports that may be required.

Disability This may affect the maintenance for children if the child is disabled, or if any of the parties are disabled. In the divorce it is one of the main factors to be taken into account.

Divorce A legal process in ending a marriage.

Domestic proceedings A general term for divorce, property and children matters.

Domicile The country in which you are normally living. It is a technical legal question, which affects your ability to ask the court to decide on your marriage. It is normally where you regard as your permanent home.

Duress Any force imposed upon another without their consent.

Enforcement A procedure whereby the court arranges for the court order to be carried out.

Emergency protection orders Under domestic violence there are various emergency protection orders which may be applied for.

Engaged couple Couple who are intending to get married.

Equity Usually described as fairness, but also can be described as the difference in the value of the home, property and any loans that are upon it.

EU law Ultimately all British courts are to observe EU law.

Evidence Proof that will be required by the court in any court case. There are strict rules of evidence.

Family law A general term covering divorce, children, etc.

Father Normally the natural father of the child, but they have different rights whether they are married or unmarried.

Financial disclosure That which is required in the procedure for ancillary relief.

First appointment in ancillary relief proceedings Once an application is made for ancillary relief there are various appointments that are set with a view to resolving outstanding matters.

Five facts in divorce The various facts which support the contention of irretrievable breakdown.

Hearing A general term for any appearance at court.

Inheritance Tax Act 1975 The current level for paying inheritance tax is £285,000, but the current (2006) Chancellor has said it will increase to £325,000 over the next four years. Any sum left over that is subject to 40% tax.

Interim order Order that the court may make during the continuance of the proceedings before the final order.

Judicial separation The same grounds applied to judicial separation as for a divorce. Fairly rare.

Kidnapping See abduction.

Legal Aid A system whereby those not on sufficient income can obtain finance to proceed with their case. This is subject to the statutory charge.

Lump sum payments Payments paid out of capital, rather than maintenance which would be paid over a period of time.

Magistrates' court Various applications can be made into the magistrates' court, which is part of the criminal system.

Maintenance Payments made to the spouse under certain conditions.

Marriage The formality of becoming married which must adhere to strict guidelines.

Martin order An order made by the court as a result of the Martin case. Mrs Martin required somewhere to live and the court decided that the house could not be sold for 20 years so the sale of the property was deferred.

Matrimonial Causes Act 1973 A current act under which current divorce is the subject.

Matrimonial home The home where the husband and wife live, as a married couple.

Mediation Usually a third party gives independent help to solve differences between the parties.

Mesher order Another order delaying the sale of the matrimonial home.

Molestation Behaviour which annoys another, can include violence and threats.

Mortgage Using a property under freehold or leasehold as a security for a debt.

Non-intervention principle The principle whereby the courts do not normally intervene in matters of children; they may try to get the parties to agree themselves.

Non-molestation order An order by the court to prevent the applicant being molested.

Occupation The right to remain in the matrimonial home.

Parental responsibility Automatically rests with the natural mother and married partners, subject to an agreement of a court order for an unmarried father.

Paternity The social and legal acknowledgement of the parental relationship between a father and his child.

Petition (divorce) A petitioner is the person who makes the application for the divorce or judicial separation. A petition is served on the respondent.

Polygamy Being married to more than one person at the same time.

Prayer The petition which asks the court to make orders in favour of the petitioner.

Pre-nuptial contract Agreement made prior to the wedding concerning what will happen if there is a breakup of the marriage.

Prohibited steps order Order which may be made in relation to children.

Rape Sexual intercourse without permission.

Reconciliation certificate A certificate produced by a solicitor as part of the petition process.

Registrar Former name for the district judge. The lowest rank of judge who sits in the county court.

Residence order An order made by the court as to where the child is to live.

Respondent The person of whom the petition is served – that is, the opposite of the petitioner.

Same sex partners Now covered by Civil Partnership Act 2004.

Section 8 orders Cover a range of orders such a contact order, prohibited steps order, residence order and specific issue order. All matters relating to the children.

Section 41 appointment The court will decided whether the arrangements for the children are adequate.

Separation agreement An agreement between the parties not to live together.

Service The methods by which the petition, notices of application, orders and decrees are supplied to the parties concerned.

Solicitors' Family Law Association A group of solicitors who have agreed to abide by certain guidelines.

Special procedure divorce case In an undefended divorce, the decree can be issued without either petitioner or respondent having to appear (or be represented) at the court.

Specific issue order An order under the Children Act resolving some particular dispute about the children's upbringing.

Spouses Parties to the marriage.

Standard procedure divorce The normal divorce which does not rely on any court appearances is a standard undefended divorce.

Statement of arrangements for children For children. Documents that need to be served on the court with the petition.

Statutory charge Anyone on legal aid may have a charge put on their property to cover the legal aid costs that have been incurred usually on a freehold or leasehold property.

Tenancy The right to live in the property for a certain period.

Variation of order An application to the court to vary the previous order.

Useful Addresses, Websites and Forms

www.hmcourts-service.gov.uk

www.hmrc.gov.uk:inland revenue

Bar Council, Complaints Department, 289–293 High Holborn, London. Tel: 020 7242 0082. www.barcouncil.org.uk

Child Support Agency www.csa.gov.uk

Council of Mortgage Lenders, North West Wing, Bush House, Aldwych, London WC2B 4PJ. Tel: 0845 373 6771. Fax: 0845 373 6778. www.cml.org.uk

Department of Works and Pensions www.dwp.gov.uk

Divorce Registry www.hmcourts-service.gov.uk

Institute of Legal Executives www.ilex.org.uk

H M Land Registry www.landreg.gov.uk

Law Society of England and Wales www.lawsociety.org.uk/ home.law

Law Society of Northern Ireland www.lawsoc-ni.org/

Legal Services Commission www.legalservices.gov.uk Non-departmental public body that administers the Community Legal Service (previously Legal Aid), and The Criminal Defence Service.

Legal Services Ombudsman www.olso.org

Relate www.relate.org.uk

FORMS

Her Majesty's courts service website www.hmcourts-service.gov.uk sets out all the current forms/leaflets that you will require. There are currently 62 forms and guidance notes. All of them are downloadable on to your computer so that you can print them off. Some county courts and the Principal Registry of the Family Division in London deal with divorce and other family cases. If your local county court does not handle divorce applications the staff will tell you the nearest county court that can help.

Stage 1 Starting proceedings
About Divorce (Leaflet D183)
I want a divorce – what do I do? (Leaflet D184)
Children and divorce (Leaflet D185)

Stage 2 Response
The respondent has replied to my petition – what do I do? (Leaflet D186)

Stage 3 Decree nisi
I have a decree nisi – what must I do next? (Leaflet D187)

This breaks down the three main stages of a divorce logically.

Appendix: Letters and Forms

STARTING DIVORCE – CONCILIATORY LETTER TO SPOUSE – UNREASONABLE BEHAVIOUR

To spouse/respondent if petition is based on unreasonable behaviour.

Dear [   ]

I have decided that unfortunately the best course of action for us is that there be a divorce.

Obviously I have to establish one of the five facts, and I have decided to proceed on the grounds of unreasonable behaviour.

I have drafted a petition of divorce setting out the details.

If you could kindly approve it and return it to me I will arrange for the petition to be served on the court.

Yours sincerely

STARTING DIVORCE – CONCILIATORY LETTER TO SPOUSE CONCERNING ADULTERY

To the spouse – concerning adultery

Dear [ ]

I have decided that unfortunately the best course of action for us is that there be a divorce.

I have decided to proceed on the basis of your adultery with another woman.

It will not be necessary for us to name her in the divorce papers.

Could you kindly confirm that you agree to a divorce on that basis.

Yours sincerely

LETTER TO SPOUSE ENCLOSING STATEMENT OF ARRANGEMENTS FOR CHILDREN

Dear [ ]

As no doubt you are aware one of the documents that is required by the courts is a Statement of Arrangements for the Children. This is just to set out the arrangements that are being made for the children under the age of 16 or under the age of 18 still in full-time education.

I enclose a copy of the Statement I have prepared and the courts do prefer if both parents agree to the arrangements.

If you agree to the arrangements could you please sign it on the last page where indicated so that I can forward it with the petition.

Yours sincerely

LETTER TO SPOUSE CONFIRMING TWO YEARS' SEPARATION

Dear [ ]

I have decided unfortunately to proceed on the basis of having been separated for two years and I am writing to see if you would be prepared to divorce on the basis of that fact.

Could you kindly confirm that you agree to a divorce on that basis.

Yours sincerely

LETTER TO SPOUSE CONFIRMING FIVE YEARS' SEPARATION

Dear [ ]

As you know we have been separated for five years.

Would you please kindly confirm that you agree to a divorce based on the five-years' separation.

Yours sincerely

LETTER TO RESPONDENT SERVING PETITION

Dear [ ]

I now enclose by way of service a petition [Statement of Arrangements for Children] and Acknowledgement of Service form.

You will need to complete the Acknowledgement of Service form and return it to the court saying whether you agree to the divorce, within eight days of receiving this letter.

Please let me know once you have done this.

I look forward to hearing from either yourself or any solicitor instructed by you.

Yours sincerely

LETTER TO THE LAND REGISTRY ENCLOSING NOTICE OF SEVERANCE SIGNED BY ONE JOINT TENANT ONLY

Dear Sirs

[   ] District Land Registry

Title Number [   ]

Address [   ]

I enclose a certified copy of a Notice of Severance sent to the other registered proprietor on [   ], together with a copy of my letter of the same date to that registered proprietor. I have not received a reply to that letter.

Yours faithfully

LETTER TO OTHER JOINT TENANT SEVERING JOINT TENANCY

Dear [ ]

I enclose by way of a formal service a Notice of Severance.

Please acknowledge safe receipt of this letter and sign and date the enclosed Notice of Severance and return it to me as soon as possible.

Yours sincerely

LETTER TO LAND REGISTRY ENCLOSING NOTICE OF SEVERANCE SIGNED BY BOTH JOINT TENANTS

Dear Sirs

To the [   ] Land Registry

Title number [   ]

Address [   ]

I am the registered proprietor of the above property and enclose a Notice of Severance signed by both registered proprietors, and request that you register us as tenants in common restriction accordingly.

Yours faithfully

SPECIMEN PARTICULARS OF THE PETITION

Desertion

The respondent has deserted the petitioner for a continuous period of two years prior to the presentation of this petition.

Particulars

On [date] the respondent after a quarrel with the petitioner said that she no longer loved the petitioner and had no desire to continue living with him.

On the following day the respondent packed her personal clothing and left the matrimonial home, saying that she did not intend to return and thereby evincing an intention to bring cohabitation permanently to an end. The petitioner gave no cause for such separation and did not consent thereto.

The petitioner and the respondent have lived separate and apart since the said date.

Specimen particulars of two years' separation and consent

The petitioner and the respondent have lived apart for a continuous period of at least two years immediately preceding the presentation of this petition and the respondent consents to a decree of dissolution of marriage.

Particulars

On or about [date] the petitioner and the respondent ceased to have sexual relations with each other, having agreed that they had nothing in common which justified their continuing to live together and that their marriage had irretrievably broken down.

On [date] the petitioner and the respondent ceased to occupy the same bedroom and to perform any domestic tasks or other tasks for each other.

Since that date they have maintained completely separate households, albeit under the same roof.

OR

The petitioner and respondent separated on [date] when the petitioner left the matrimonial home and have never since then resumed cohabitation.

OR

Where there has been a subsequent resumption of cohabitation:

From and since [date] the petitioner and the respondent have resumed living together for two periods not exceeding six months in all, namely from [date] until [date] and from [date] until [date].

Specimen of five years' separation
The petitioner and the respondent have lived apart for a continuous period of at least five years immediately preceding the presentation of this petition.

Particulars
The petitioner and the respondent separated on [date] when the petitioner left the respondent since which date they have never resumed cohabitation [save between [date] and [date] being a period of less than six months].

Specimen particulars of intolerable behaviour

The respondent has behaved in such a way that the petitioner cannot reasonably be expected to live with the respondent.

Particulars

Assaults

The respondent has a quick temper and has frequently assaulted the petitioner.

1. On the [date] when the petitioner was watching television and was struck on the head and face.

2. On the [date] petitioner was about to go to work and the respondent threw plates at his head.

Drunkenness and insulting behaviour

1. The respondent was drunk to excess and despite of all his requests she has not moderated her drinking.

2. Because of the drink the respondent has become abusive to the Petitioner and to the children, to their great distress.

Failure to maintain

1. Throughout the marriage the respondent has kept the petitioner short of housekeeping money and on occasions provided no housekeeping money at all. He has used the housekeeping money to gamble and run up considerable debts.

2. The respondent has incurred large debts as a result of reckless and extravagant spending and is constantly receiving letters and phone calls from creditors, who threaten to take proceedings in respect of such debts.

LETTER TO COURT ENCLOSING APPLICATION FOR FILING PETITION – EXEMPT FEE

Dear Sir or Madam,

I am acting for myself in this matter and I take this opportunity of enclosing:

1. Petition with copy of service
2. Statement of arrangements for children with copy for service
3. Marriage certificate
4. Application for fee exemption

I look forward to hearing from you in due course with confirmation that the petition has been served on the respondent.

Yours faithfully

LETTER FILING PETITION WITH FEE

Dear Sir or Madam,

I am acting for myself in this matter and I take this opportunity of enclosing:

1. Petition with copy for service
2. Statement of arrangements for children
3. Marriage certificate
4. Certificate with regard to reconciliation
5. Cheque in the sum of £ [   ]

Please return the issued proceedings to me for me to effect service on the respondent. I look forward to hearing from you in due course.

Yours faithfully

ACKNOWLEDGEMENT OF SERVICE

A N Other

Number of Matter

BV [number]

In the *Any Town* County Court

Between

Mr A N Other
Petitioner

-and-

Mrs X N Other
Respondent

This is the exhibit marked 'A' referred to in the Affidavit of the Petitioner
Mr A N Other

Made [date]

Before me

Form M7(b)

FAMILY PROCEEDING RULES

Rule 2.24(3)

Affidavit by petitioner in support of petition under Section 1(2)(b) of
Matrimonial Causes Act 1973

In the *Any Town*   County Court*
                                                 Principal Registry*

Delete as appropriate

No of Matter BV[number]

Between   *Mr A N Other*

And   *Mrs X N Other*

QUESTION	ANSWER
About the Divorce petition 1. Have you read your petition in this case including what is said about the behaviour of the respondent?	
2. Do you wish to alter or add to any statement in the petition or the particulars? If so, state the alterations or additions	
3. Are all the statements in the petition and the particulars, including any alterations or additions, true?	
4. If you consider that the respondent's behaviour has affected your health state the effect that it has had on it.	
5. (i) Is the respondent's behaviour as set out in your petition and particulars continuing? (ii) If the respondent's behaviour is not continuing, what was the date of the final incident relied upon by you in your petition?	

In the [name]	* County Court
Case No. *Always quote this*	BV[number]
Applicant's solicitor's reference	
Respondent's solicitor's reference	

**Ancillary relief
Cost estimates of
Respondent**

Marriage of *Mr A N Other* and *Mrs X N Other*

Part 1

	Prescribed rates for publicly funded service (£)	Indemnity rate
1. Ancillary relief solicitor's costs (including VAT), including costs of the current hearing and any previous solicitor's costs		
2. Disbursements (*include VAT as appropriate and any incurred by previous solicitors*)		
3. All counsels' fees (including VAT)		
TOTAL		

Part 2

4. Add any private client's costs previously incurred (*In publicly funded cases only*)		
GRAND TOTAL		

Part 3

6. State what has been paid towards the total at 5 above		
7. Amount of any contributions paid by the funded client towards their publicly funded services		

NB If you are both publicly funded and might be seeking an order for costs against the other party complete both rates.

Dated:

LETTER TO COURT REQUESTING DISTRICT JUDGE'S CERTIFICATE

Dear Sir

I am the petitioner and accordingly enclose:

1. Request for directions for trial
2. Affidavit in support of petition

I look forward to receiving the district judge's certificate in due course.

Yours faithfully

REQUEST FOR DIRECTIONS FOR TRIAL LETTER TO THE COURT

Dear Sirs

Re: Our Client *A N Other*

We act for the petitioner and accordingly enclose:

1. Request directions for trial
2. Affidavit in support of petition

We look forward to receiving the district judge's certificate in due course.

Yours faithfully

EXAMPLE OF DECREE NISI

IN THE [   ] County Court

        BETWEEN   Mr A N Other

        AND   Mrs X N Other

Before District Judge [   ] sitting at [   ] County Court

On the [   ]th [   ] xxxx

The Judge held that

The respondent has behaved in such a way that the petitioner cannot reasonably be expected to live with the respondent.
That the marriage solemnised on [   ]th [   ] 19xx

At rhe Register Office in the District of [   ] in the County of
[   ]

Between Mr A N Other

And Mrs X N Other

Has broken down irretrievably and decreed that the said marriage be dissolved unless sufficient cause be shown to the court within six weeks from the making of this decree why such decree should not be made absolute.

> Notes
>
> This is not the final decree. Application for the final decree (decree absolute) must be made to the court. (For guidance see leaflet D187 'I have a decree nisi – what must I do next?'

LETTER TO COURT ISSUING RESPONDENT'S ANCILLARY RELIEF PROCEEDING

Application to the Court for Ancillary Relief

Dear Sirs,

Re: *A N Other – v – X N Other*
                       No of Matter – BV[number]

I enclose for issue, Form A in triplicate.

I also enclose our cheque for £[   ] in respect of the issue fee.

Please return the two sealed copies of Form A for service upon the mortgagees and Notice of First Appointments.

Yours faithfully

LETTER TO THE COURT FILING FORM E – FINANCIAL STATEMENT

The Court Service
Anytown County Court
Anytown
Blackshire

Dear Sirs,

Re: Case No
   A N Other – v – X N Other

On behalf of the petitioner, I enclose for filing Form E sworn on [date].

I confirm that I have served a copy on the respondent's solicitors.

Yours faithfully

LETTER TO THE OTHER SIDE'S SOLICITOR REGARDING THE FIRST APPOINTMENT

A N Other
Any Road
Blank Town
Blankshire

Dear Sirs,

Re: Our client – A N Other
Your client – X N Other

I refer to the above matter and enclose by way of service a copy of my financial statements with exhibit.

I confirm that I have received a copy of your client's financial statement.

Yours faithfully

LETTER TO OTHER SIDE'S SOLICITOR CONCERNING COSTS IN READINESS FOR FIRST APPOINTMENT

A N Other
Any Road
Blank Town
Blankshire

Dear Sirs,

Our Client: A N Other
Your Client: X N Other

I refer to the above matter and enclose by way of service, my client's costs schedule in readiness for the first appointment hearing list in the [name] County Court on the [date].

I would be grateful if you would acknowledge receipt.

Yours faithfully

LETTER TO COURT ENCLOSING APPLICATION FOR DECREE ABSOLUTE

Dear Sir

I am the petitioner and I enclose an application for decree nisi to be made absolute together with my cheque in the sum of £[   ].

I look forward to receiving the decree absolute.

Yours faithfully

LETTER TO COURT ENCLOSING CONSENT ORDER

Dear Sirs

We enclose, by way of application for consent order:

1. Petitioner's Form A
2. Respondent's Form A
3. Petitioner's Form M1
4. Respondent's Form M1
5. Consent order plus duplicate clean copy
6. [Notice of acting]
7. Cheque for £[   ] by way of fee

Please place this letter before a district judge.

We look forward to receiving the consent order as soon as possible.

Yours faithfully

PRECEDENT CONSENT ORDER – RECITALS AND UNDERTAKINGS

IN THE

[   ] COUNTY COURT   Matter No:..........

BETWEEN:

A N OTHER

and   Petitioner

X N OTHER   Respondent

CONSENT ORDER

UPON the Petitioner and Respondent agreeing that the terms of this Order are accepted in full and final satisfaction of all claims for income capital and pension sharing Orders and of any other nature whatsoever which either maybe entitled to bring against the other or the other's estate howsoever arising.

AND UPON the Petitioner and Respondent agreeing that the contents of the former matrimonial home known as *Any St, Anytown COXX 1XX* (the property) shall remain the absolute property of the party in whose possession they now are.

AND UPON the Petitioner and Respondent acknowledging and agreeing that the former matrimonial home known as *Any St, Anytown COXX 1XX*, was sold on [date] at a sale price of £[   ].

AND UPON the parties acknowledging that in consideration of the agreement reached it is not the respondent's intention to make a referral to the Child Support Agency.

AND UPON it being acknowledged that from the net sale proceeds the Petitioner received a sum equivalent to 45% of the net proceeds of the sale of the property defined as the gross sale of £[   ] less mortgage redemption figure of £[   ], estate agents' commission of £[   ] and solicitors' fees of £[   ] only in addition to 45% of any monies received for fixtures and fittings.

AND UPON it being acknowledged that from the net sale proceeds as defined above, the Respondent received the balance monies equivalent to 55% of the net sale proceeds in addition to 55% of any monies received for Fixtures and Fittings.

BY CONSENT IT IS ORDERED THAT:

1. The Petitioner is ordered to assign within 56 days from the date of this Order to the Respondent her interest in *Any St, Anytown COXX 1XX*.

2. The Petitioner is ordered to assign within 56 days from the date of this Order to the Respondent her interest in the *Any St, Anytown COXX 1XX*.

3. The Respondent is order to pay or caused to be paid to the Petitioner the sum of £[   ] within 56 days of the date of this Order.

4. Upon completion of the sale of the property and payments to the Petitioner of the sums referred to in Paragraphs Numbered 3 and 4 above as provided for by Recital 3 of this Order and upon the making of a final Decree herein the Petitioner's and the Respondent's claims for financial provision pension sharing and property adjustment Orders to stand dismissed and neither the Petitioner nor the Respondent shall be entitled to make any further application in relation to their marriage under the Matrimonial Causes Action 1973 Section 23 (1) (a) or (b) or to make an application to the Court on the death of the other for provision out of his or her estate.

5. There be no Order as to costs insofar as the Application and the negotiations ancillary thereto are concerned.

6. There be liberty to apply as the implementation and timing of the terms of this Order.

Dated this   day of   200X

. . . .

Blank Solicitors   Blankety Solicitors

Blank St   Blank Rd

Anytown   Anywhere

County Cxx 8xx   County Pxx 2xx

. . . .

Respondent   Petitioner

LETTER FROM SOLICITOR TO CLIENT ENCLOSING DECREE ABSOLUTE AND WHAT HAPPENS NEXT

A N Other
Blank St
Blank Road
Blanktown

Dear Client,

I now enclose your decree absolute dated [   ] which you should retain in a safe place as this document replaces your marriage certificate.

I advise you that now you are divorced you should check your National Insurance position.

From now on various benefits will depend on your own contributions and you should therefore consider whether you wish to pay the full rate of National Insurance Contributions.

These benefits include Contribution-based Job Seekers Allowance, Sickness and Incapacity Benefit and your retirement pension.

I suggest that you check the position with the relevant authority and make any amendments which are necessary.

Please note that divorce affects pension rights.

If you have a will, you should review it now.

My firm can help you with the preparation of a new will. Please let me know if you would like me to contact you about making a new will.

The charges for preparing the will are based on the time spent and the usual fee for preparation of a straightforward will is about £[   ] plus VAT.

Please note that if you remarry any existing will is automatically cancelled and of no effect, meaning that if you die your estate will pass in accordance with the laws of intestacy.

You will probably no longer be entitled to a widower's pension under an occupational or private pension scheme. As far as the basic state pension is concerned, if you have not yet reached retirement age you can select to use all your former wife's National Insurance contribution records instead of your own if this would entitle you to a higher state pension.

If you are already retired and you are receiving a state pension, you will continue to do so at the same level at which you are receiving it now.

If you select to choose your former wife's contribution record for your own basic state pension, please note that if you remarry before you reach retirement age you will lose your entitlement to use that record and your basic state pension will instead be based on your own contributions record or on the contributions of your new wife.

Therefore if you contemplate remarriage just before you reach retirement age and you want to preserve your right to receive your basic state pension based on your former wife's National Insurance contribution records, you should consider delaying the wedding until after you have retired since it could make a significant financial difference to you.

Please let me know if you want me to explain this further.

I also advise you that divorce affects inheritance.

If you do not have a will, you should make one now.

Yours sincerely

CONSENT ORDER

IN THE [   ] COUNTY
COURT

                                        Matter No: [   ]

BETWEEN:

A N OTHER

                                          Petitioner

                      And

X N OTHER

                                        Respondent

CONSENT ORDER

Blank Solicitors
Blank St
Anywhere
County
Cxx 1xx

Ref: PRW
Solicitors for the Respondent

TRUST DEED IN RELATION TO FREEHOLD PROPERTY

Relating to how the property will be held if someone who has put money towards the purchase price is not on the title deeds.

This will give them the right to share in the property on the sale.

THIS DECLARATION OF TRUST is made the [   ] day of [   ]
Two Thousand and [   ]

BY [   ] and [   ] both of [   ] in the County of [   ]
(hereinafter called 'The Trustees')

WHEREAS

1.   [   ] is the registered proprietor of [   ] which is registered under
      Title Absolute Number [   ] (hereinafter called 'the property') and is
      holding the same as sole proprietor for an Estate in fee simple

2.   [   ] will hold the property on behalf of the Trustees as tenants in
      common

The Trustees desire that as from the date of this Deed they shall hold
the property as tenants in common

NOW THIS DEED WITNESSES AS FOLLOWS
1.   The Trustees declare that as from the date of this Deed they will hold the
      property upon trust for themselves as tenants in common

IN WITNESS whereof the parties hereto have executed this instrument
as a Deed the day and year first before written

SIGNED as a DEED by the said)
[   ] in the   )
presence of:)

SIGNED as a DEED by the said)
[   ] in the   )
presence of:)

DEED OF CHANGE OF NAME

Dated [   ]

DEED OF CHANGE OF NAME

[   ]
SOLICITORS

THIS DEED OF CHANGE OF NAME is made the [   ] day of [   ]
20[   ] by me the undersigned [new name] formerly called [old name]
of [address] a British citizen.

1.   I was born on [d.o.b.] and I am divorced.

2.   I on behalf of myself wholly renounce, relinquish and abandon the use of
     my former surname [   ] and in place of it I assume my birth surname of
     [   ] so that I will from today be called, known and distinguished not by
     my former surname of [   ] but by my birth surname of [   ].

3.   I shall at all times from today in all records, deeds and writings in all
     proceedings, dealings and transaction private as well as public and on all
     occasion use and sign the name of [   ] as my surname in place of and in
     substitution for my former surname of [   ].

4.   I therefore expressly authorise and request all persons at all times from
     today to designate and address me by my birth surname of [   ].

Signed as a Deed by the above-named

[new name]
Formerly [   ]
In the presence of

Witness signature
Witness name
Witness address

Witness occupation

CALDERBANK LETTER

At any stage you are entitled to make a proposal to the other side with a view to reaching or settling an agreement.

The letter is written in accordance with the Calderbank principle, that the proposals are trying to reach an agreement that may not be produced at the court at the final hearing.

The district judge will consider the favourable terms of the offer and pay the costs from the date which they could have reasonably accepted the offer.

These offers are usually made after the full disclosure has been made.

Calderbank letter to other party's solicitors

Dear Sirs

WITHOUT PREJUDICE SAVE AS TO COSTS

I have now had the opportunity to consider this matter carefully and in an effort to compromise this matter and to avoid the necessity of a full hearing in court I am prepared to put the following proposals for settlement.

1. That the former matrimonial home [   ] be placed on the market for sale at the best possible price.
2. That the net proceeds of the sales be divided as to [   ] and [   ].
3. The settlement shall be in full and final satisfaction of all or any claims that either party may have against the other under the Matrimonial Causes Act 1973, the Married Women's Property Act 1882 or any other relevant legislation.

4. That neither party shall be entitled to apply against the estate of the other under the Inheritance (Provision for Family and Dependants) Act 1975.

5. That there be no order for Costs (save public funding assessment).

If the above is agreed I would suggest that it should be incorporated into a consent order to be approved by the court.

I reserve the right to refer this letter to the attention of the court should any issues arise as to costs at any future date in accordance with the principles described in Calderbank – v – Calderbank.

Yours faithfully

Index

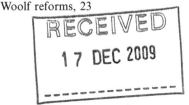